INDIAN VILLAGE FOLK

INDIAN VILLAGE FOLK:

Their Works and Ways.

T. B. PANDIAN

GYAN

Published by

Gyan Publishing House
5, Ansari Road
Daryaganj, New Delhi-110002
Phone: 011-47034999, 9811692060
E-mail: books@gyanbooks.com

Distribution Network
gyanbooks.com
India, USA, Canada, UK, Australia, France

ISBN: 978-81-212-8676-3 (PB)
First Published, 1897

2nd Impression 2023

Printed at: Gyan Press, Delhi.

INDIAN VILLAGE FOLK
Author: T. B. Pandian

INDIAN VILLAGE FOLK.

T. B. PANDIAN.

INDIAN VILLAGE FOLK:

Their Works and Ways.

BY

T. B. PANDIAN,

AUTHOR OF 'ENGLAND TO AN INDIAN EYE,' ETC., ETC.

LONDON:
ELLIOT STOCK, 62, PATERNOSTER ROW, E.C.
1897.

CONTENTS.

I.

THE VILLAGE.

II.

TRADES, ETC.

III.

PROFESSIONS.

IV.

PUBLIC LIFE.

V.

LEISURE HOURS.

APPENDIX.

LIST OF ILLUSTRATIONS.

INDIAN VILLAGE FOLK.

I.

THE VILLAGE.

1. THE HOUSEHOLDERS.

SOME idea of a village house in India will be given in the chapters describing the different handicrafts. It is proposed to begin this book with a faithful account of the habits and customs of the inmates of a village house in a tropical climate. To give a clear idea of the actual life of the people, it will be necessary to describe carefully a selected typical house. All the dwellings in a village are built in the same way; and though there are serious disadvantages in the method of construction, the houses are precisely adapted to the needs of those who have to live in a hot country.

The house of Mr. Raman lies in the centre of a village called Puttupore. Its walls are built of sunburnt bricks and clay, and its roof is covered with palmirate palm-leaves. It has two outer *pials* facing the street, one on each side of the main entrance. Immediately on entering we find an open hall, which is known as the *koodam*. In this hall male visitors are received, and the inmates of the house meet and chat together in leisure hours. It is also used as a bedroom for the elderly members of the family. After an open space of about fifty feet in circumference we come to the house proper, which faces the north, and has a large hall, a store-room, and a kitchen. The hall is used both as a dining and sleeping room, and there is seldom any furniture to be seen in it, save a common village cot in one corner, and a few mats and pillows rolled up and kept in another corner. In the storehouse are the provisions for living preserved in earthen vessels, and the clothes and other valuables of the inmates. In the kitchen are various earthen vessels needful for cooking, and the brass pots and vessels which are used for eating and drinking. Near the kitchen there is a doorway which leads into a back yard. This is used as a kitchen-garden, and has in it drumstick-trees, peas, greens, pumpkins, cucumbers, onions, etc. On the eastern side of the house a cattle-shed is placed, and in this the cows, bullocks, and buffaloes are sheltered. All these buildings are encircled with mud walls, in which there is only one opening, and this is available for both man and beast. The apartments kept for the use of the inmates receive the light and air only through the doors, as there is not a single window in the entire building. There is, however, quite sufficient provision for free ventilation through the bottom of the roof.

The inmates of the house get up very early in the morning. The male members of the family go for their morning ablutions, and while they are away the female members sprinkle cow-dung over the outer and inner yards, and occupy themselves in sweeping the house, and cleaning the cooking and eating vessels. In their turn they then march to the watering-places, where they bathe themselves, and wash their clothes, and bring water home for family use. The morning bathing is not, however, universal among all the classes of the village community.

In the house of Raman there are two females, Raman's wife and his mother. When they have returned from the watering-place they attend to the work of feeding the men, and preparing for the noontide meal. About eight o'clock in the morning Raman and his brothers come in for their morning meal, which is generally some cold rice, with butter-milk, and some pickle or chutney, or some cold sauce. Having taken their morning meal, the superior creatures of the house leave in order to attend to the cultivation of the land or other works. As soon as the men have finished their meal the female members help themselves to what is left of the dishes.

In taking their meals they all use the floor as their table, plantain-leaves or brass vessels as their plates, and their hands as spoons.

Following the female members in their daily routine, we find them busily engaged in pounding the rice and grinding the curry-stuff, and dressing a few vegetables and greens in preparation for the noontide meal. Between twelve and one o'clock the men return home hungry, and then there is placed before them a sufficient quantity of cooked rice, with some vegetable sauce, greens, and pulse—not to mention the attendant butter-milk or curd. The men cheerfully partake of this simple village-meal, and then go to their outer hall and chew betle-nut. Then the females take their noontide meal; after which they rest for an hour, or even two, and during this time the men and the women converse together on common topics of the village. At about four o'clock the female portion begin to occupy themselves with preparations for their evening meal, and in arranging the household things. At six o'clock Raman's wife places a light in a hole, which is prepared for the purpose in the wall, and then prostrates herself before the lamp, and smears a small quantity of ashes on her forehead. The other members of the house on first seeing the lamp do the same. About eight o'clock the men take their supper, which usually consists of some pepper-water, rice, and vegetables, and the remainder of the sauce that was prepared for the mid-day meal. The female members follow the men in taking their supper, and all the eating for the day is over by nine o'clock, and then they all retire to bed. One day's life of Raman and his family is a picture of all, for only slight differences are made even on festival days.

It is common among the women of the village to make their own *virattees* (lumps of dried cow-dung) for their fire-places; and they are also engaged in their leisure hours at the country spinning-machine. Sometimes they go to the fields, and assist at the work which is being done by the labourers. In the family of Raman it is the mother who generally does the outdoor work, his wife attending to the duties of the house; and this is generally the case when the mother-in-law and the daughter-in-law live together. It is a very common thing to find uncomfortable relations prevailing among the village mothers-in-law and daughters-in-law. Perhaps ten out of a hundred mothers-in-law live peaceably with their daughters-in-law, but 90 per cent. quarrel incessantly. Sometimes they may even be seen fighting like beasts of the field, using vulgar language, holding in their hands each other's hair, and pelting each other with mud or stones. Still, it must be understood they are not to be regarded as enemies until their death. To-day they fight one another, to-morrow they laugh together. One day's fighting does not destroy another day's peace. If the male members interfere at all in this fighting, they generally take the part of the daughter-in-law. This sad condition of things is largely due to the ignorance of the villagers, and the absence of all culture of self-restraint. When education is introduced, a better state of things will be developed in the rural districts of India.

GRINDING CURRY POWDER.

Observing the varied duties and claims of our friend Raman, we cannot fail to admire the laborious spirit of this village cultivator. He is busy with many things. He has the care of his family, as he is the head of his house; and he has to direct his farm-labourers and his brothers in attending to the work of the field. He must answer to the different calls of the village officers. He is invited to a wedding or to a funeral in his own village, or to some distant village where he has relatives or friends. On some of these joyful or sorrowful occasions he takes his wife with him. Sometimes, if he is ill or otherwise engaged, he sends his wife or mother with one of his brothers to represent his family. There are many calls on Raman's poor purse. The priest, the beggars, the poets, the pious, the village policemen, the weddings and the funerals of his relatives—all of them have a share in Raman's earnings.

2. THE INN.

The people who live in the Indian villages take delight in giving alms to the helpless and the needy, and also to the religious mendicants who go from place to place on pilgrimage, begging as they go. They have also provided suitable and convenient places in which travellers and strangers may rest, without any charge being made for their accommodation. These inns are called *chatiram*, *oottoopuray* and *maddum*.

The *chatiram* is a place built by a Hindoo king or chief, by one of the Hindoo governors of former times, or by some wealthy Hindoo man or woman, or by a certain class of the Hindoo community, and it is usually sufficiently endowed for its maintenance. These buildings are generally large and spacious, having separate apartments for cooking, sleeping, etc. They are placed outside the village, and usually near a stream. To provide bathing and cooking for the travellers, a well is dug by the side of the *chatiram*, and the grounds are planted with fruit-bearing trees and flowering plants. In some of these *chatirams* the authorities engage Brahmin cooks, who supply with food a certain number of Brahmin travellers only, each day free of charge. In some *chatirams* the travellers are both fed and housed entirely without charge, but in others the travellers get their lodging free, but have to provide their own food. When wealthy men or women find that there are no children to inherit their property, they lay out the whole, or at least the greater portion, in building and endowing *chatirams* for the public good. These charitable institutions may be numbered by the hundred in the country districts of India.

In the villages of Travancore, the 'land of charity,' there are sixty-four *oottoopurays*, *i.e.*, 'feeding-houses,' established by the ancient Hindoo kings of Travancore, and still maintained by the Maharaja of Travancore in quite a grand style. In these 'feeding-houses' the Brahmins are fed by the hundred every day with sumptuous meals, and they are provided with other comforts at the expense of the State of Travancore. Many homeless and helpless Brahmins subsist by travelling from one feeding-house to another, and in this way they spend the whole year in quite an enjoyable manner, without any care as to 'what they shall eat, or what they shall drink, or wherewithal they shall be clothed.'

The simplest and plainest kind of charitable public lodging is called the '*maddum*,' and this is built in many instances at the expense of the villagers themselves. In these *maddums* a poor man, who has some reputation for piety, is engaged as manager by the villagers. This man gradually becomes an ascetic. He clothes himself in an orange-coloured tokai, and is called *sanniasin* by every villager. The duty of this *sanniasin* is to see that the village inn is kept clean, and lighted regularly every evening. He has also to beg meals from the villagers, both morning and evening. A certain portion of the meals thus collected by the innkeeper is taken for his own use, and with the remains the poor travellers are fed.

If any respectable travellers come in to rest, either for the day or for the night, the innkeeper gives them all necessary attention, and he will even at times induce some rich villager to feed the strangers who may have come in late at night. The lighting of the inn is left to the well-to-do villagers, and they supply the lamp-oil by turns. The clothing of the innkeeper, which is, however, but a little matter, is provided from the village 'general fund.' The organization of the village inn is quite simple and inexpensive, and the benefit derived by the travellers is very great. During the hot summer months the innkeeper supplies butter-milk or cold water to the thirsty travellers who are proceeding on their way.

There are a few famous and well-established *maddums*, with their *madāthipathies*, *i.e.*, 'governors of inns,' which were originally established on the simple principle of the village inn. Now these remarkable *maddums* have grown enormously, and are large establishments with numerous supporters and followers. The most prominent of these inns are called *dharmapura maddum*, and *tiruvādoothuray*. The governors of these celebrated Hindoo inns established a brotherhood of Hindoo monks, and these monks became the heads of the respective inns; they are, as a rule, sound vernacular scholars, and well versed in Hinduism in all its phases. They maintain celibacy. These inns have four or five hundred men who feed in their respective places, where their disciples and visitors flock together in large numbers. The heads of these are not Brahmins, and so they are not exclusively kept for that caste. The non-Brahmin community, indeed, form the bulk of their supporters. The insolvent and broken-down merchants, and those who have become disgusted with life through various disasters, forsake their homes and relations, and enter this brotherhood of Hindoo monks; they are then cared for all the days of their life. Some of those who join this society are sent out by the head of the establishment to represent their cause at their branches. All those who become governors of these inns are vegetarians by birth and Sivites by religion, and their successors are trained and kept in readiness by the governors. Although the governors themselves are bachelors who have not much earthly enjoyment, as they try to show, yet their relatives are greatly benefited by their honoured and exalted positions. They spend the money out of the treasury of the inn just as they please, and sometimes in very profligate ways. They live in princely comfort, and their intelligence and culture give them a high position and influence in the Hindoo community. Some of them are really enlightened men, and these come to the front and sympathize with public movements, more especially those of a religious and educational character.

There is no doubt that these inns and other charitable institutions of India will work wonders, if only the organizers of these institutions and their governors will recognise the fatherhood of God and the brotherhood of man.

3. THE CLOCK.

The villagers are men of simple habits, and they often make good use of things which are natural and inexpensive. To regulate the business and the orderly movements of the villagers, there is no such thing as a clock-tower in a conspicuous position, or even a clock or timepiece in the villagers' homes. It is quite a novelty to see a watch in the hands of a villager. However, they have their own clocks, timepieces and watches, and these are found in the blue sky, in the open fields, and in every orderly household arrangement. Probably there is no class of people in the world who get up so early as the Indian villagers do.

Some of these timekeepers have wonderful alarums in themselves, and these help the villagers to get up punctually at appointed hours of the night in order to attend to their respective occupations. By looking at these clocks they also register the exact times of the births of their children, in order to help the astrologer in writing out their horoscopes. In this way the lucky hour is found in which to perform the marriage ceremony.

The first and most inexpensive clock is the *sun*, the light-giver, whose movement is watched through the day by different classes in the village community in order that they may properly attend to their work. When the sun appears to the villagers as the dayspring, those of them who attend to the work of supplying flowers to the village temples, and to the villagers, set out for their gardens in order to pluck their flowers. The female portion of the village show themselves to the goddess of ill-luck, who is supposed to have waited before the door all the night. They drive her away by sprinkling cow-dung over the front and back yards of their houses; they also immediately engage in sweeping their houses, cleaning their cooking utensils, and their eating and drinking vessels.

When the sun has risen to a certain height (9 a.m.) the villagers call it *āhdoo yalumbugira nārām*, *i.e.*, the hour at which the sheep get out of their folds. This is the general time appointed by the villagers for seeing one another on business; this is also the time for the village schoolmaster to send the children for their morning meals. When the sun is in the middle of the sky (12 a.m.) the villagers have their noon-tide meal, whether they stay in the house or labour in the fields.

When the sun sets the villagers bring all their active work in the fields to a close. The shepherds turn their sheep into the folds, the village priests go to the temples to offer evening prayers and sacrifices to the village gods, and the children rush out from the school and make their way homewards with their books on their backs. At all other times the villagers measure their shadow in order to find out the exact hour; and they do this even for the satisfaction of the traveller, who may have a handsome watch in his pocket which keeps correct time.

During the night there are several timepieces which enable the villagers to find out the exact hour in which to attend to their business, if they have any. When the silver light of the moon shines on the quiet and retired village, it assists the inhabitants in finding out the time; when the moon disappears by natural causes, the shining stars play the part of a timepiece through the night, and the villagers call these stars by different names. One of them is called *Āram Köottam*, a group of six stars, and the position of the group denotes a certain time of the night. By observing the movement of these stars the richest and the poorest villagers attend to their duties in the night. The morning star leads the business of the village. The farm labourers set out to feed their cattle, and they get ready to start to their fields at the first appearance of the morning star. They talk to each other thus: 'Valli yalumbittoo!' *i.e.*, 'The star has risen, hurry on!' The priest makes his way to the temple to awake the gods by blowing the holy shell (*shankoo*); their parents awake schoolboys to get ready for the school; the men who work at the village water-lifts start their work of drawing water from the wells to feed the vegetables, plants, and greens. The songs which these men sing are called *yāthapáttoo*, and amuse the travellers who are passing at that time from village to village, often carrying heavy burdens; and the Brahmin priests start off to the neighbouring villages to receive their incomes from the villagers by attending to some ceremonies; mothers put their babes in their cradles, and sing in praise of their darlings, or in praise of their gods or departed relations, and so put their babes to sleep. This gives them time to attend to their early-morning duties and to go for the water. The shepherds leave their flocks and herds in the fields in charge of dogs and young lads, and go home to take their morning meal, and to bring food for the dogs and for the lads, and also to fetch grass, or certain herbs with which to feed the tender and lame sheep. Just at this time the hunters go and hide themselves under the bushes between the jungle and the fields, in order to shoot deer and antelope, which are returning from the fields to the jungle; and the oilmongers start off with oil-vessels on their heads to sell their oil in the distant hamlets.

The villagers decide to do certain work at twelve o'clock in the night, or to start off to some distant place to attend to some business, or to take part in a festival of a famous temple, at three in the morning. Then exactly at twelve the first alarm is given by the cock—the village clock—beating its wings loudly, and thus calling to the slumberers to awake from their sleep. Again, at three, a number of these village clocks give their continued and loud alarms, and raise the sleeping folks. While the most expensive clocks often become speechless and useless through some little mistake in the works, the village clocks strike hour by hour systematically and punctually.

During the time when the thick clouds are passing and heavy rains are falling, the celestial world is darkened, and life in the village becomes dull and inactive. But through the chill and cold of the Indian winter the blackbirds fly to and fro, and in and out of the villages, and announce the dawn of day with their strong voices. These are sure winter clocks, and of a matchless kind to a humble community.

4. FIRE IN AN INDIAN VILLAGE.

There are from one hundred to a thousand houses in each village of India. Almost all of them are built with mud walls, and covered with thatch roofs. The streets are narrow, and the houses are very close to each other. The low roofs and the light building materials cause great calamities whenever a fire breaks out.

There are times in which the houses are burnt to ashes by accidental fires, which are caused by carelessness in cooking, or by the children playing with lucifer-matches. These accidental fires take place all the world over, and no special reference need be made to such cases. When we refer to village fires we mean the periodical fires which take place during every summer month, and which cause great damage to property, and even loss of life.

These periodical fires take place in almost every village, and are serious evils. Houses are destroyed, straw and hay are consumed, and the villagers are often left without homes, and their cattle without food. There is no fire brigade; there are no fire-engines, or even water-pumps, that can be used to bring the fire under control.

Other houses are situated in the open plain, without any shelter from the westerly winds, which bring dust-storms, and add to the flames, and swiftly spread the conflagration all over the village. When the fire takes place in the day-time, most of the villagers will be away in the fields, and they become alarmed at the sight of volumes of ascending smoke at a distance. The men rush back at once to their village, and the females follow them; but their efforts are all in vain; before they can reach home they find their grain, pulse, cotton, hay, straw, clothes, and all their other belongings, burnt to ashes; they have to be thankful if their children have not also perished in the flames. Who can describe the deplorable condition of the villagers whose houses are thus burnt, with all their belongings? The poor creatures become homeless; they remove the ashes, and make an effort to live within the shelter of the burnt, bare walls. There are no philanthropic persons in these villages, such as are found in Western countries, who will come to the rescue of such homeless folk. The Government cannot possibly give any help. So the only alternative for these poor people is to borrow money from well-to-do men of their village, or of the neighbouring villages, and spend it in rebuilding their homes. When this is done they may go on smoothly for a fortnight or so, only to have their houses burnt down again. Then they are really broken down. However, they try their best to affect another loan, and put up their thatched roofs. Having done this, all the villagers are set upon watching to find out who it is that has done the mischief. While they are watching day and night, and waiting carefully to catch the enemy, the fire gets in some western corner of the village, the high wind carries it round till all the houses are burnt down, and the third time the home goes. Alas! their hearts are melting; tears are running down their cheeks from their eyes; the men curse their gods, and behave as savages to one another; the women beat their breasts, and cry aloud; the children become mournful and disorderly—everything goes crooked, and the poor villagers are completely ruined. It takes a long time to recover from such heavy blows. In some villages there are fires almost every day for about two to three months. Fire here, fire there, is the cry continually. When one house takes fire, the people jump on the roofs of the other houses, and rapidly uncover them, in this way preventing their houses from catching fire. The fire also takes place in the heaps of palm-leaves and straw with which the houses are covered. When the villagers see that the fire mischief has commenced, they unroof their houses, and live exposed under the burning sun during the day time and in the heavy dew of the night. It can easily be imagined what it is to live in the summer time under the burning sun without a roof.

During our short stay in Palumcottah we saw fires almost every day in some direction of the village. The harmless and simple-minded shepherds lost many of their houses, and the remaining few had their roofs uncovered. As it is a place where there is a strong police force, we heard the fire-bell ringing every now and then. During the whole months of February and March, the fire-bells were ringing almost every day. These bells went, on an average, six or seven times a day. If we stood outside the village, on an elevated place, which would give a view of five miles around, on dark nights we could see flames of fire either in the village houses or in the field-stacks.

It is simply extraordinary to observe that these fires in the villages appear periodically every year, *without any attempt to check them.* This adds to the money troubles of the poor cultivators, who have many other drains on their purses. It is said that if a set of thieves enter into a house in the night they will leave some things behind them which they consider to be of no use to them; but when a fire takes place in a house it burns down everything and spares nothing. We know that the great fire of London stamped out the terrible plague in the year 1666. Out of the ashes of her burning the mighty and enterprising Chicago has risen again; but out of the ashes of the Indian villages which are burnt in these periodical fires only more poverty, a harder struggle for existence, and pressing hardships of life have arisen.

Having stated some features of village fires, we shall now proceed to investigate their causes. There are different opinions prevailing. The first and foremost opinion of the village people is that it is *yaaval, i.e.*, the action of a devil. Some enemy of the village—*tattapary*, for instance—engages a famous wizard or witch, a native of Travancore, and pays him or her a large sum of money to induce his or her 'familiar' to set fire to the houses of that village. It is said that the wizard or witch occupies a house somewhere in the neighbouring village, and sends the devil to do the mischief. The amazing part of it is that generally the fire begins at the top of the roof of the house. If the fire is put out at an early stage, then the people discover a round ball of cloth, from which the fire originated ; and, still more amazing, when the people are engaged in trying to put out the fire, other fires break out in two or three houses in another street, and all at the same time. Within five minutes there is a fire in two or three houses in the western street, and this makes the ignorant mass to believe that it can be nothing but the action of the devil.

Perhaps our readers may be interested in the theory of engaging a devil even to do the most menial service. It is this : If a man desires to get a devil to be his *yāval—i.e.*, servant—who will do anything for his master, he must undergo certain ceremonies and master certain *mantrams*, *i.e.*, charms. First of all, he must have a sloth, and he must also be a man of undaunted courage, strong will, and great physical endurance. He must spend a whole Friday in fasting and praying, and then he must take the sloth in his left hand, and must proceed to the cremation-ground, which is far away from the village. As soon as he arrives at the ground he takes the water from the eyes of the sloth and applies it to his own eyes. Then he sees an army of small devils assembled on that cremation-ground, each holding a rod of office in his hand. They all come round the man to tease and frighten him, and they will do him all kinds of mischief. Some devils pull his nose, some his hands, some his legs, and some his long hair. If the man is at all frightened by the threats and troubles of the devils, they will kill him on the spot. Whilst the fight is going on in this way between the devils and the man, the man is trying to gain his object. So he sharply snatches a rod from one of the devils. At once all the devils go a stone's throw away, and hold a meeting among themselves. The chief among them issues an order to all the devils to the effect that the devil who lost his rod will not be admitted into their community, and he will be looked down upon as one who has lost his office, his connection, and his relationship until he regains his rod. By this time the man who has got the devil's stick makes his way towards home, with the devil following, teasing, and frightening him. But the man is firm as a rock. Then the devil begs and cringes to the man, beseeching him to hand the rod back to him; but all in vain, the man will not yield an inch to the devil, and goes home, and keeps the rod in his safe box, shutting it with padlock and key. The devil waits at the gate as a slave, ever ready to obey the man's orders. Now is the chance for the man to do anything he likes through the devil. He can get the fruits of the mountains in five minutes' time; he can get sweets, flowers, scents, and any eatables; but the man must pay the price of the articles, so that the devil may take it along with him to fetch the articles. And this devil will also set fire to a house if he receives orders to do so from his master. Whenever the man wants a thing to be done, he takes hold of the devil's rod in his hand, and issues the order to the devil, who immediately proceeds to perform it.

There is a class of people called *purada vannans*, *i.e.*, washermen for the out-caste people. Some of the men and women of this class are supposed to be notorious wizards and witches. They cannot read or write their vernacular language, and they are as a class very ignorant. Whenever this people send word to a village they get what they want. In fact, they tax the poor villagers to give them an annual contribution. If any villagers refuse to give this tax, the next day the fire commences in the village. There was a famous woman belonging to this class of people who was known as 'Fire-setting valli.' She was simply a terror to the villagers. She had a regular perennial harvest from them. If she sent word to the oilmongers, oil came to her ; if she sent word to the shepherd, he brought her sheep and lambs ; if she wanted anything from the gardeners, they supplied her with any quantity of vegetables. Of course, all these things were free of charge. These wizards and witches frighten the people to the best of their ability ; and they use phosphorus in order to set places on fire in a way that cannot be readily discovered. There is quite an art in engaging certain rascals to do this devilish trick.

There are quarrels and divisions also among the villagers, and one party will set fire to the houses of the other party. What is joy to a jackal is death to a lamb ; and when two of the villagers are trying thus to ruin each other, there is untold misery in store for all the village folk.

Whatever may be the causes of these fires, one thing is certain : many poor, harmless, and innocent people are made to suffer beyond measure annually by the brutal action of the rascals who indulge their resentment by burning the houses of their neighbours. The law of the land is very strict, and when these 'little devils' are found they are severely punished, but they often escape without being caught.

II.

TRADES, ETC.

(MEN WHO LIVE BY THEIR HANDS.)

1. THE WASHERMAN.

WESTERN people have very imperfect ideas of the Indian washerman. Most of the families in the West either do their own washing at home, or send it out to a laundry. There is no separate class or caste of people that does the work of cleaning the clothes and ironing them. Anyone who takes to this work may take his place in society if he has the necessary learning and accomplishments. The son of a washerman may freely move in good society, and take his stand among men of light and learning. Nobody will look down upon him because he happens to be the son of a washerman. He may marry the daughter of a wealthy merchant, and even become a member of Parliament in England, or a Senator or a Congressman in the United States of America. In the course of years his children may become members of the best society in the land in which they live. Sufficient wealth and advanced education, together with a certain amount of knowledge of the 'art of living' with others, can make the descendants of a washerman take rank as ladies or gentlemen; but nothing of this kind can happen in the case of the washermen of the villages of India. The term *vunnan* is taken from the Sanscrit *varnam*, which means 'colour' or 'beauty.' There are 140,000 washermen in Southern India alone. In Malabar the females of this class wash the clothes, and the men have taken to the trade of tailoring, or to the profession of devil-dancer.

The *vannan* is called, in consideration of his innumerable and unscrupulous services, 'the son of the village.' He washes all the clothes of both the men and women, his wife assisting him in some parts of his work. When she goes to fetch the clothes from the women's apartments, the women of the house receive the 'daughter of the village' warmly, and entertain her with interesting conversation for a few minutes; then they give her a little oil with which to anoint her head, and feed her with a cold meal. Sometimes they also give her some home-made cakes to take back with her to her children. The washerwoman leaves the house highly pleased. She carries the soiled clothes of the women hooked on a stick, lest she should be contaminated by the touch of them. She takes the things to the fuller's ground, at a pool, or river, or tank, and submits them to a regular process of cleansing. First she throws each article into the water and sets it aside. Then she herself plunges into the water, in order to remove any defilement which she may have contracted in the process. She then places all she has collected in the heap of other soiled clothes from the village which her husband has brought. The *dhoby* (washerman), as a rule, does not consider himself to be polluted in ordinary cases when he carries the soiled clothes.

The *dhoby* has his house in some corner of the village, and it is built on a piece of ground belonging to the village. The walls of his house are raised at the expense of the village people, and they themselves pay for the thatched roof. They also contribute to the purchase of a spirited donkey or two. Of useful household articles the *dhoby* has hardly any; only a few earthen vessels in which to cook his food, and to serve for washing purposes. His business apparatus consists of only a few large earthen pots, and these are filled with water and placed on an oven, which is built of mud, and in a triangular shape. This oven is heated whenever he wants the soiled clothes to be steamed. Before they are steamed he dips them over and over again in alkaline water, which is obtained by him at very little cost. This alkaline water is nothing more than a mixture of pure water with fuller's earth, or washing-soda. When the process of steaming is done, the *dhoby* and his children start off at about four o'clock in the morning to the fuller's ground. The poor, uncared-for donkeys move about in the dull streets and waste lands of the village all the other days and nights except the night in which the *dhoby* intends to start for his work. The unfed beasts are then made to carry the heavy loads of wet clothes. The moment they are loaded they start off in advance from the house of their unkind master, as they know well the place of destination, and the way to it is quite familiar to them. The *dhoby* with his children follow them, each carrying a heavy load on his back, and even on his head. As the *dhoby* passes through the streets he cheers his beasts by whistling, and uttering encouraging words such as these: 'Poda sami,' *i.e.*, 'Go, master'; 'Manum kappata,' *i.e.*, 'Save my reputation'; 'Kartua thoraya,' *i.e.*, 'black gentleman'; 'Addyada singar,' *i.e.*, 'Walk as a lion.' When he reaches the water-side—and this is often a good distance away—first he throws off his own load, and removes the loads off the backs of his beasts, and then the donkeys are left to find their own pasture.

In cases where there are fields in cultivation, one of the grown-up children of the *dhoby* minds the brutes while they are grazing. Then the *dhoby* unties the bundle of clothes, and keeps them within his reach near water, where the rough stones are kept, for bleaching. He takes up a cloth in his hand and dips it in the water, and beats it against the stone, with an invocation to his God, the common Father. Then he places the cloth on the stone, and raises his right hand to his forehead, as he stands in a bending attitude, in order to indicate that he seeks the benediction of Heaven to rest upon the labours of the day.

The work of a *dhoby* in an Indian village is tedious and difficult. He has to cleanse from two to three hundred cloths of various lengths and breadths, many of them in an exceedingly dirty state. He beats cloth after cloth with his full strength on the coarse stones. His children also share the work of their father, taking for their part the tiny clothes of children like themselves.

While he is beating the cloths he sings songs of his own making, or that were made by his forefathers. These are very peculiar in their composition, and they are quite uninteresting to anyone beside himself. There is in them no melody, and there is not even any beating of time. He sings in praise of his ass, or of his wife, or he narrates his love, patience, earnestness, in relation to his sweetheart before his marriage. Sometimes he sings in praise of his father-in-law. Sometimes it is a mournful song about an old and faithful ass which he has recently lost.

While the *dhoby* is busily engaged with the washing of the clothes, his wife will turn up carrying a potful of cold food, which she has been obtaining from the village folk during the previous night. Every house in the village is bound to give twice daily a handful of cooked food, either made of rice, millet, maize, or some other Indian grain. She also carries a second small vessel, which is filled with cooked Indian vegetables and greens. These have also been given to her by the villagers.

THE WASHERMAN.

A *dhoby* receives as wages from every village house an average of sixpence per annum. If in the house there is a large family the wages are increased to a shilling per annum. Besides this allowance, he gets a small gift of grains, probably a few measures, at the time of harvest. If he goes to the fields when they gather the crops, he also will get a small bundle of ears. At wedding festivities and at funerals he is entitled to a fee of fourpence. When the villagers offer a blood-sacrifice to the bloodthirsty gods, they generally kill a fat ram by severing the head from the body, and this head goes to the waiting *dhoby* as a part of his wages. In some villages the *dhoby* is used as a messenger to communicate ominous intelligence to the parties concerned. For this he gets, in the form of gold and silver bangles, or a pair of new cloths, or a pagoda, about the value of four shillings. This is all that the *dhoby* receives in the form of wages.

Now let us turn back to the place where we left the *dhoby* washing the clothes. He has been beating them against the stone, one after another, from early morning until 10 a.m., and he is now quite exhausted, and quite ready for his morning meal. The wife, who has brought his meal, joins her husband, and the children also partake of it. They all sit on the grassy slope of the riverside or pool. The *dhoby* and his children sit facing the woman, who holds the earthen pot in her hand. They fold their hands together, so as to serve them instead of a cup, and the watery meal is poured into their hands. The woman first stirs up the contents of the earthen pot with her right hand, and adds some butter-milk and salt. This luxurious food satisfies the tired and hungry *dhoby* and his children, and refreshes them so that they cheerfully resume their work. The woman, after serving the meal to her husband and children, supplies her husband with betel-nut, and chunam and tobacco to chew. The *dhoby*, having received these, sits beside his wife, and gossips with her, while she helps herself to the remaining food. When she has done the *dhoby* lays his head on her lap and rests awhile. She relates to him some incidents of the village life which have recently come to her knowledge. In half an hour the *dhoby* and his wife, with their children, get up to resume their work. They hurry on the bleaching of the clothes till 2 p.m.; then they begin to wash the beaten clothes in a large earthen pot, which is filled with pure water. In this a small portion of indigo is dissolved, or a little piece of lime. In this mixture all the clothes are dipped and rinsed well. Then they undergo another process of dipping in a similar pot filled with water, in which a small quantity of starch, prepared from rice or other Indian grain, has been put. This process makes the clothes somewhat stiff. All these processes cleanse the clothes very thoroughly. If the clothes are new they have to go twice through all these processes, and in addition to this they are also dipped in water mixed with cow-dung or goat-dung. This process gives the clothes a smart appearance.

Most of the villagers wear white clothes, consisting of a pair of cloths of three or three and a half yards each. Some of them have also turbans or headpieces.

As the day is getting on the *dhoby* and his wife and children now hurry off to dry the clothes, either on grassy meads or on sandy banks. At about three o'clock the *dhoby* and his family go up together to some shady banyan or tulip or margosa or tamarind-tree; one or other of these is sure to be found near an Indian village. Here they partake of the remainder of the meal, seated in the manner which has been described. At about five o'clock they gather together the clothes and fold them up. Now the children go to find the donkeys, who are to carry the loads of bleached clothes back again to their home. The *dhoby* and his wife themselves carry bundles of the clothes on their heads and on their backs; they go slowly back to their village.

The following morning the *dhoby* and his wife unloose the bundles of washed clothes, and arrange them for delivery; both of them are very busy making up the piles according to the marks on the clothes. As a rule, the *dhobys* in India are very skilful in sorting the clothes according to the marks given them. There is no such thing as the marking of the clothes by their owners with coloured threads or the initials of their names. All marks on clothes are made by the *dhobys* themselves, and they cannot usually write their own names. If any one of the villagers is in a hurry for his bleached clothes he has to go to the door of the *dhoby* and fetch them for himself. Generally, the *dhoby* delivers at each house.

The Indian villagers never use linen or any form of dress that is made by tailors, and therefore there is no need for ironing.

The *dhoby* not only washes the clothes of the villagers, but he also provides them with torches, made out of the rags which he gathers and stores up from the worn-out clothes given to him. These torches are generally used in festival and marriage processions; and he also renders service by holding the torches on such occasions. The *poor* people of the village, by courting his friendship, get from him *marthu*, *i.e.*, the loan of cloths for little or nothing. At the time of funeral processions he spreads cloths on the way leading to the cremation ground. His services are also sought to decorate with cloths the roof of the marriage pandal or booth. On all these occasions he uses the cloths of the villagers. When the village dramas are held in the open-air at night he spreads on the ground a few bleached white cloths for the more respectable men of the village to sit upon.

The 'son of the village,' who is fed by the villagers, has also the privilege of clothing himself, as well as his family, with the clothes of the villagers. To-day he turns up in a new attire which he has got from Mr. A—— for washing; similarly his wife shines in the borrowed feathers of Mrs. C——. To-morrow he walks in the street with the clothes of Mr. C——; and likewise his wife appears smart and tidily dressed with a beautiful *sari* or draping belonging to Mrs. R——. On the following day the husband and wife will carry all the clothes in which they dressed themselves on the previous day to the fuller's ground, and will cover themselves with their worn-out ordinary clothes in a state next to rags. If any of the owners see these common children of the village wearing their clothes they take no notice of it. The village *dhoby*, who has this privilege of wearing other people's clothes, has also the free use of the village clothes as his bedding. It is evident, therefore, that it costs little or nothing to maintain himself and his family.

The fuller's ground becomes the centre for several village *dhobys*, and to it the young unmarried men and the young maids go to wash the clothes of their respective villages. These young people have thus fine opportunities of knowing one another better, and of forming close friendships. They cannot, however, have private conversations about their matrimonial affairs. Supposing the young man A—— has a tender regard for the young maid C——, he sings some love songs while beating the clothes, and in these he describes to the best of his abilities the position, parentage, and beauty of the girl who probably stands close beside him, also beating clothes. These love-songs of the young *dhoby*, who is quite taken up with the girl whom he has in his mind, have a charming effect upon the girl, and she in return raises her sweet voice with songs of allurements. She assures him in an indirect way of her appreciation, alluding to his personal beauty: 'O thou young man, black as oil, strong as stone, sweet as sugar-cane, I cannot ever forget thy face. Thou hast become the subject of my night-dreams. Whenever I think of thee I become useless to do the work of my parents. Thy love makes me uneasy in the day and restless in the night. My mother has promised to give me the young and beautiful colt as my dowry, and my father has promised me the right of washing the clothes of the whole village when he gets old and helpless, as I am the only daughter to my father. I saw thy foot-print and the foot-print of thy black donkey. When will the day come in which I may get a handful of betel-nuts from thy hands?'

When the young man hears these songs it is enough to break his heart, and he sings out loudly, assuring her of his burning love for her, calling her *thana* (honey); *mana* (deer); *annama* (O swan!); *purava* (O dove!). 'Thy love kills me. I can give my four donkeys as a price for thee. I will work for thy father and for thee all the days of my life. If I have thee in my house there is no need for a light. O thou dove! in still waters on my left-hand side show me thy face to remove the gloom of my thoughts.' Thus the young *dhoby* and the maid sing out the songs of love at their meetings at the washing-ground. When the parents of these young folk see their attachment to each other, they arrange to have them settled in marriage, and to follow the profession of a village *dhoby*.

The washermen are a distinct class or caste. The son of a washerman is a washerman by compulsion. He cannot follow any other trade but the trade of his forefathers. He cannot intermingle with other classes of people, as this would be opposed to the social customs of the country.

2. THE CARPENTER (*Taccthan*).

The carpenter is one of the five useful artisans of the village. The people of a large village usually have a carpenter living in their midst. But when the village is small, the carpenter has to take up the work of other villages in order to secure a sufficient maintenance. He makes the yoke and other wood implements for ploughing, the handles for hoes, spades, axes, weeding tools, sickles, and other necessary implements for agricultural purposes and for the irrigation of land. He makes ornamental door-posts, and also doors, rafters, plain bedsteads, wooden spoons, and stools of various sizes for domestic use. At the time of village festivals, according to the requirements of the occasion, he makes portable cars or stages, for taking the idols in procession. Several of these mechanics unite in making a portable temporary car, at a cost of 1,750 rupees, for the temple of Madura every year. All the temples of India have large and magnificent ornamental cars, which can only be drawn by thousands of men, and these are made by the skilful carpenters. Images of different kinds and forms are also made by the *taccthan*. He makes village carts for the conveyance of passengers and loads. He gets in the form of wages a certain number of bushels of grain from each farmer; and, as usual, he also gets a bundle of corn, and certain measures of grain, at the harvest time.

But he makes a separate charge for constructing carts, vehicles, doors, and doorposts.

He wears a sacred thread on his shoulders, like the other artisans. His wife never helps him in his manual labours. There are 31,237 carpenters in Southern India alone.

In a certain large village there was a carpenter who was celebrated for his artistic skill, especially in making wooden images. He had shown good taste in this direction from his boyhood; he had attracted the attention of the other artisans when he was but a boy of fourteen. His fame went abroad as a renowned carving carpenter, and several of the native village chiefs, hearing of his reputation, sent for him to their respective places, and got him to do work for them. When the work was accomplished they would present the young carpenter with gold bangles and other ornaments, besides money gifts, in order to indicate their esteem for him, and their appreciation of his skill. In course of time the young carpenter became very popular, and enriched himself by his artistic abilities. One summer morning this carpenter happened to pass through a street in which a Roman Catholic priest lived. The carpenter, out of curiosity, went into the church, and there noticed some of the images that had been made in France. He declared that he could make images equal to any of these. At once he was brought to the notice of the priest, who asked him to make an image of St. Xavier out of the trunk of a solid tulip-tree, and promised him a handsome present if he did it well. The carpenter, having consented to do the job in a month's time, went to his home and commenced upon the work. Some six months before a Hindu had given him a large trunk of a tulip-tree, from which he wanted him to make an image of one Karuppana Sawmi, a blood-thirsty village god. The carpenter, having executed that work, kept the remainder of the wood, and now found it very serviceable to him. With great care and skill he carved the image of St. Xavier, and presently took it to the priest, and received his reward. The priest then arranged for the festival of the saint. A grand procession was formed to carry the image through all the streets of the village. Amongst the other spectators was that Hindu who had given the wood to the carpenter. In the midst of this great procession this Hindu, who had no distinct ideas about religious matters, shouted out in the very midst of the people, 'Ah, how nice the image looks! Is it not the younger brother of our Karuppana Sawmi, the village god?' The enthusiastic Catholic worshippers beat him severely for uttering such defiling and blasphemous words. The Hindus then rose against the Catholics who had beaten the Hindu, and so there was a great commotion and uproar in the village.

On the following day they brought a charge before the nearest magistrate against the Hindu who had blasphemed their saint. The magistrate, on investigation, found out that the Hindu was an ignorant man, and that, in his ignorance, he believed St. Xavier, the great Jesuit missionary, the forerunner of their mission, and Karuppana Sawmi, one of the many tutelary Hindu gods, were really brothers, as both these images had been made out of the one piece of tulip-wood which he had given to the carpenter. The carpenter was summoned to give evidence before the magistrate. The magistrate, being a Hindu himself, laughed at the idea of image-worship prevailing among a certain class of Christians, and dismissed the case, saying to the Roman Catholics, 'Your image is no better than the Hindu image.'

Among the carpenters there have been several renowned

poets who distinguished themselves at different periods in India. One of them was the great Suppra thepa Kavyrayer, a poet, and a contemporary with Father Beschi; and it is he who, after his nominal conversion to Catholicism, helped Beschi in composing 'Tembavani,' a poetical work in High Tamil literature, containing a graphic and descriptive account of the Holy Land, Palestine.

3. THE BLACKSMITH (*Kullan*).

As India is an agricultural country, the services of the blacksmith and carpenter are indispensable. The village blacksmith generally has a circuit of his own. If a blacksmith lives in a village called Pandiapuram, he has several other villages attached to it, and does the work also for them. If a village is a large one, he may limit his labours entirely to it. In some smaller villages the carpenter does the work of the blacksmith as well as his own. During the time of ploughing the blacksmith finds it difficult to meet all the demands of the villagers, for he must make iron blades for their ploughs, and repair their old ones. He also supplies the villagers with heel-tips, hinges, hooks, locks and keys, axes, knives, sickles, spades, crowbars, 'uramonuis,' *i.e.*, kitchen-knives; choppers, 'panaarooval,' *i.e.*, reaping-hooks; and other useful implements. Some blacksmiths have their workshops under trees, while others have theirs in thatched huts. The blacksmith has a few hammers of different sizes, a bellows, and some pincers, and with these instruments he works to the satisfaction of the villagers. The workshop of the blacksmith is usually crowded with men who have come in from other villages belonging to the circuit of the blacksmith, in order to get their implements repaired or new ones made.

The ironsmith is not such a schemer as the village goldsmith, but he will take his own time in doing his work. Indian villagers are seldom in a hurry, and the ironsmiths are very fond of chatting with the people who bring their work to them. The blacksmith is, in truth, a great gossip, and delights in fishing out every secret of the village.

This chatterbox goes to his work about 7 a.m., and returns home late in the evening. If a villager comes to him to sharpen an axe, say at about 8 a.m., he is kept in the workshop till 5 p.m. During this time the ironsmith will try his best to waste his visitor's time by introducing vain conversation, and endeavouring to extract news from him. To begin with, he desires to know how Mr. A—— is getting on; how Mr. D—— and Mr. C—— have settled their dispute; why Mr. G——'s cow died; why Mr. F—— sold his big bullock; why the girl B—— is not married; when are they going fishing in the Western Tank? Do not you know that the sea-fish is very cheap now?—such things as these begin wearying conversations. The poor villager, who has been actually starving, at last takes up his axe and walks home, having waited about the workshop nearly the whole of the day. The work of sharpening a worn-out axe should not take more than an hour.

As a rule, the smith never goes to fetch work, and never returns it to his customer. The villagers always bring their own work to the workshop, and take it back when it is finished. In many cases they will have to wait in his workshop day after day, and watch him doing the work for them. He is all the day away from the village, working in his lonesome workshop. If he has any male members of his family he makes them assist in his work, but the female members never help him. One of them brings him his noonday meal to his workshop.

In the form of wages, the ironsmith gets a fixed fee from every house, which varies according to the position of the tenants. There are others who pay at once for the work that is done for them. The cultivator usually engages his services for the whole year, and gives him a fixed allowance, as well as special gifts, such as a bundle of ears at harvest time, and a few measures of grain, and some money, on the occasion of important festivities.

Some of the ironsmiths are well versed in the vernacular of the country, and have a general knowledge of the works of their poets. One day, a certain Tamil poet came to a blacksmith's workshop with the intention of getting some help from him. As soon as the poet entered the workshop the blacksmith said: 'Varum pulavara erumbadium'—*i.e.*, 'Come on, poet, sit down and sing.' The latter word, 'erumbadiam,' has two meanings; the one is, 'sit down and sing,' and the other is, 'sit down and beat the iron.' The poet misunderstood the ironsmith, and gave the latter meaning to the word; so he showed an unpleasant countenance. Then the blacksmith addressed the poet in a very courteous manner, 'Erumbadium.' At this the poet became angry, and said: 'Thou fool! don't you know that I am a poet? How dare you ask me to sit down and beat the iron!' The blacksmith for the third time begged the poet to sit down and sing, using the same Tamil word, 'erumbadium.' At this the poet became furious, and called the ironsmith 'a dog and a stupid ass.' Again the blacksmith said: 'What is the matter with you, poet? Don't be angry; sit down and sing.' But he again used the same Tamil word, 'erumbadium.' The poet now lost control of his temper, and beat the blacksmith with his walking-stick. Then the smith took one of his hot bars, and branded the poet with it in several places. Immediately a charge was brought against the smith before the chief of the village. On inquiring into the case, the magistrate pitied the ignorant poet, but punished the witty blacksmith.

There are 13,741 of this useful class of artisans in Southern India alone.

4. THE GOLDSMITH (*Thattan*).

A marked characteristic of Indian life is an excessive fondness for jewellery. This distinguishes even the lower classes of society, and it is one of the chief causes of national poverty. Hence the services of the goldsmith cannot be dispensed with in Indian villages. He is one of the five artisans of India. The men of this class do not intermarry; they have their own priests, and do not allow any of the Brahmin priests to officiate for them; but they imitate the Brahmins in all their ceremonies. Their girls must be married before they attain womanhood, and widow-marriage is strictly prohibited. The use of flesh and of alcohol is nominally forbidden. But, nevertheless, they indulge in drink, and eat fish and flesh, to a large extent. This particular class of artisans bury their dead in a sitting posture, but cremation is also practised amongst them. They have the general title of *Achari*, and some of them are called *Pattan*, which is the equivalent of the Brahmin *Bhatta*. Every village has a goldsmith, who, like other artisans, belongs to a separate and distinct class. The son of a goldsmith cannot be anything else but a goldsmith. He is unlike a *dhoby* or a barber, in rendering his services to the villagers. Money is always flowing into his hands. In some places he lives in grand style, like the landlords. He has his workshop in his own house, and his tools are a few hammers of different sizes, pincers, and tongs, a few moulds, and a furnace made out of a broken earthen vessel; with these wonderful instruments he turns out really beautiful jewellery. He makes ear-rings and finger-rings for both sexes. He also makes bangles, nose-jewels, ankle-jewels, toe-jewels, upper ear-ornaments, belts, head-ornaments, etc., and these are of good workmanship. He makes other jewels for children—*kungumany* and *aramoody*, to conceal the nakedness of boys and girls. Some make these jewels in gold, and others in silver, according to their circumstances. He employs one or two to assist him in his work, and all of them are well-trained rogues. Suppose a village goldsmith receives 150 rupees (£10) from Mrs. A—— for making a pair of gold bangles, on January 15, 1897. He assures her that she can have her jewels on February 1, 1897. He takes the money, and goes home. As soon as he reaches his house, his wife comes to meet him with a smiling countenance, to find out whether he has brought money with him. The goldsmith then gives the money to his wife, who keeps it in his box. After this he takes his meal, and sits to his work. Then his wife comes near to him, and whispers in his ears of the vows which they have to fulfil to their family gods. She says that it is very dangerous to put off the fulfilment of the vows to some future time, as she had some strange and fearful dreams last night. In fact, she says that one of her children is suffering from fever, and surely the god will be angry with him if they do not pacify him at an early date. So she readily gets the consent of her husband to the offering of a blood sacrifice to their family god. They fix an auspicious day for that purpose, and she freely makes use of the money from Mrs. A—— in purchasing a fat ram, fruits, flowers, cocoanuts, perfumes, and other necessary things. In this way she spends some 40 rupees, and the remaining 110 rupees are utilized by the goldsmith for making jewels for which he has already taken money from others, and used for his own benefit. In the meantime Mrs. A—— visits the house of the goldsmith, in order to find out what progress he has made with her jewels. The goldsmith receives her with great courtesy, and treats her with kindness. He expresses his sorrow for not being able to purchase gold of good quality, as the market has been dull for some days, and so he has sent his man to a distant town to buy some good sovereigns. With this satisfactory word Mrs. A—— returns home. About February 15 Mrs. A—— goes to the goldsmith to fetch her bangles. But now she finds the goldsmith is absent. She goes on the following day, but still in vain. She goes again and again, but she cannot find him. At last she reports the shabby treatment of the goldsmith to her husband. Now the husband goes, with the determination to take from him either the money or the bangles. This would be about the beginning of March. Now the village goldsmith is caught by Mr. A——. The goldsmith, with his usual cunning, takes out a long piece of gold which he had bought for somebody else, and shows it to Mr. A——, and begs him to exercise a little more patience—at least, for a week longer. About March 20 Mr. A—— turns up again at the goldsmith's house. Now the goldsmith has gone to a neighbouring village on some business. His wife appears, and shows Mr. A—— all the spirit that a woman can show, and pacifies him with kind words and promises, so that he consents to wait for another week. For the third time Mr. A—— goes to the goldsmith at the beginning of April, and uses harsh words, such as 'scoundrel,' 'rogue,' and 'liar' in the presence of many people. At this time the goldsmith is working on a jewel for somebody else, and this Mr. A—— appropriates as security. At last the village goldsmith finishes the bangles within three days, and takes them to Mr. A—— ; he, being satisfied with the weight and quality of the gold of the bangles, accepts them, and pays his wages—six shillings.

After some time Mrs. A—— is disposed to sell her bangles, so she sends them to market. But all those who desire to buy the jewels value them for less than four sovereigns, because they find too much copper inside the bangles. This is but an illustrative instance of hundreds of cases which occur in the rural parts of India.

The village goldsmith reaps a fine harvest when people make their marriage-tie (*tali*). As a rule, none of the villagers will care to find out the weight, or to test the quality, of the gold out of which the *tali* is made, for it is considered amongst them as a bad omen either to weigh or to find out the value of the *tali*. Hence this offers a fine opportunity for the village goldsmith to rob more than half of the gold given to him for this purpose, and to make a large addition of copper.

There are often poor people who, having given money to the goldsmith to prepare jewels for them, get tired of visiting the goldsmiths, so these men succeed in dodging them for years together.

The village goldsmiths are up to all sorts of schemes. They sometimes leave their own village and live in another village, where they show great honesty and strict punctuality in delivering jewels. Thus they gain the goodwill and confidence of these villagers, who consider *their* goldsmiths to be exceptional people of that class. Having gained the confidence of the people, the goldsmith will induce the village ladies to order valuable jewels. When he has collected enough from them he simply bolts from the village with the money. Sometimes the goldsmith works in the daytime in one village and spends his night in another village; and so he dodges about. If anyone goes to a goldsmith while he is working, he may see as many as ten persons, in an hour's time, bitterly complaining of his long delay in making their jewels.

In the case of rich and influential villagers, such as the headman of the village, or some other leader of the place, the goldsmith goes to his house, and opens his workshop there until he has finished his jewel. But here also he finds out how to dodge. He works the whole day in the house of the villager, and in the night he works in his own house, and so he finishes two jewels at the same time. Somehow he robs the villager of *his* jewel, and replaces it with his own, which he prepared in his house during the nights. The jewel of the goldsmith is nothing but a large addition of copper with gold.

Sometimes the village goldsmith gives to the people their jewels weighing more than the weight given to him. If the villager gives to the goldsmith gold weighing two sovereigns, he gives in return a jewel weighing two and a quarter sovereigns. If the villager asks why it is so, then the goldsmith demands from him extra money. But, in fact, the undue proportion of copper causes the overweight.

It is said of the goldsmith proverbially that 'thai poonneelum ma poon adduppan,' *i.e.*, a goldsmith will rob even something out of what is given him by his mother for a jewel. There is a common saying among the people that the god Siva himself is afraid of a goldsmith, and so he wears a cobra round his neck. Hence the poet sang, 'Thattanuku angee allo anninthan arran surpathayia.' It is also said that no one could cope with a *thattan* (goldsmith) in lying. The poet himself bursts out in his melody in praise of this liar, saying, 'Thattan pulukukku yatta thu kannum ratna supapatheya.'

On one occasion a high-caste Brahmin woman gave a goldsmith some money to make a jewel for her. As usual, the goldsmith delayed in making the jewel. The woman, being greatly annoyed at the long delay, went to the goldsmith's house at mid-day, and addressed the goldsmith in a rough way, and called him all sorts of names. Then she spread her upper garments on the floor and laid herself down, telling the goldsmith that she would not leave the house unless he gave her either the jewel or the money. The *thattan*, in his usual shuffling way, was working with the jewels belonging to someone else. But the woman was quietly lying down in the workshop. As the day was hot, and she was very tired, she went to sleep. Seeing the determination of the courageous Brahmin woman, the cunning *thattan* was up to his mischief. He went near the Brahmin woman, who was fast asleep, and applied the gum to her eyelids. When the woman awoke from her slumber, she found that she could not open her eyes. She cried loudly, and called to the *thattan* for help. 'What is the matter with you?' said the goldsmith. 'I find that I cannot open my eyes,' said the Brahmin woman. 'I see our goddess has made you blind. You have been abusing me all this day. I was patient; but my goddess was not patient with you, and so she made you blind,' said the goldsmith. 'Very well; what can I do?' asked the Brahmin woman. 'You should make an offering to my goddess,' replied the goldsmith. 'Yes; you can give all the money which I gave you for a jewel to your goddess and get me back my sight, as I have a large number of children and a husband to care for,' said the Brahmin woman. Immediately the goldsmith washed her eyes with cold water, and she was able to open them, and went on her way thanking the *thattan*, and thinking what a powerful goddess the village goldsmith's was.

We could multiply instances to show the cunning of the village goldsmith. But space does not permit. Suffice it to say that the village goldsmith, with all his craftiness, supplies the villagers with ornaments of excellent workmanship, and that the villagers are loaded with jewels. The village goldsmith can say, like Demetrius of old, 'Sirs, ye know that by this craft we have our wealth.'

5. THE SHOEMAKER (*Chuckler*).

One of the lowest and most despised classes is that of the poor and ignorant shoemakers. These people are found in almost every big village of the country, and they are classified as a sub-division of the Naidu caste. Their settlements are separate from the villages, as they are out-of-caste people. They live in filthy and miserable huts, surrounded with ditches and stagnant waters. They are half-naked, ill-clothed, and often emaciated. There is hardly anyone of them who can either read or write. Those, however, who have embraced Christianity are gradually making a step upwards, and are securing some education. The very hut in which they live is the birthplace of cholera and other epidemics. To add to their insanitary condition, there are holes round the huts which they utilize as tanneries. They eat the dead animals which they receive from the villagers as a part of their wages.

The shoemakers make shoes for men and women and children; they also make skin robes for the cultivators, and they are employed by the villagers as messengers and sweepers. In some places they are required to watch the cremation-grounds and the cornfields.

In the form of wages the shoemakers receive a scanty fixed annual allowance from each villager, that is, from those who are unable to pay a nominal fee for the work done for them by the shoemaker. Those who have mercy on these poor creatures give them some food, and make them cut firewood, and attend to their kitchen-gardens.

The marriage ceremonies of the shoemaker class are unusually interesting. When a young man wishes to be married his party take a bottle of arrack to the intended bride's house and give it to the father to drink. If he consents to the proposed marriage, he gives another bottle of arrack in return for the bridegroom's father to drink, and then an astrologer is consulted to secure his opinion as to an auspicious day for the intended marriage.

A parisam of six and a quarter rupees, one kotta of cholem, five measures of rice, and some oil, with saffron and cocoanuts, should be taken to the bride's house, together with a string of beads and an *olai*. The bridegroom's sister should carry some of these on her head. The string of beads is then tied by the bridegroom's sister on the bride's neck. This is the *thali*. From this day she is considered a wife. Then for five panams taken out of the parisam arrack and other spirits are bought. Both parties drink freely of these spirits.

On the *muhurtha* day a vessel full of milk is brought, and all the relations of the bridegroom take handfuls of it and pour it on the bridegroom's head, and his friend rubs it well in. After he has bathed in cold water, he is taken outside the village to a place where there is an auverei-plant (*Cassia auriculata*). Three little sticks are placed so as to form a triangle, and a potful of rice is cooked between the three sticks, which are supposed to represent a little hut. The bridegroom and his relations partake of the food.

The bridegroom then starts for the residence of the bride, but stays somewhere outside the village while the bride bathes in the same way as he has done. The bride is then taken outside the village, where the bridegroom is waiting, and there at the side of an auverei they place two sets of three sticks as a hut for each of them, and there they cook food. Their respective uncles take a handful of rice, wave it round their heads, and throw it behind them, to avert the evil eye. The remaining rice is eaten by the entire company, with the bride and the bridegroom.

The bride is taken round the huts three times by her uncle, who also places her right hand in the bridegroom's left.

Then both the bridegroom and the bride are taken to the house of the bride. While going there the bridegroom's sisters wave a lighted camphor before the bride, and receive money from her father or brothers.

Then in the front of the house the bridegroom sits on a stool with a cloth on it, and the bride pours water on him. The bride then puts on the same cloth and sits down, and the bridegroom pours water on her, and thus both bathe.

In the same place the bridegroom makes a plough of two sticks and ploughs the ground, which is wetted with the water in which they have bathed, and the bride takes *conjee* to him in a pot. She also takes a little child with her, which she gives to the bridegroom, who kisses it and returns it.

After this two or three rings are cast into a pot of water, and they both are made to take them out with a view to ascertain which of them will in future have power over the other.

Then they both are taken into the house. When entering they dip their hands near the doorposts inside into a salt-pot by way of amusement, and the bridegroom's relations beat the bride by way of a joke.

The marriages of this caste are conducted with brawling and noise, owing to the quantity of spirits consumed on the occasion, and they do not hesitate to divorce each other even for trifles. I have known a man of this caste to be married three times to different women during a single year.

6. THE BARBER (*Kuddymaken*).

The village barber, as well as the *dhoby*, is known as the 'son of the village.' He has no shaving-saloon as the barber has in Western countries; he provides no chairs of any kind for his customers.

His appliances are very few; he has no soap or even brush; he never carries Rodger's razors nor Sheffield scissors; French perfumes are not used by him; German hair-oil is not in his stock; he has neither hairbrush nor comb, but for all that he is the village barber, and he thinks that he knows his business well. He glories in his own skill; he has a few rough-made iron razors with very little of steel about them, a rusty pair of scissors, a tiny brass cup to hold water, a small piece of iron sharpened at the end to pare the nails of the fingers and toes, a thorn extractor, a coarse pincer, a rough bone, and an old piece of leather. These are the instruments which he uses for his work.

The barber, like the *dhoby*, lives in a corner of the village. His house is also built at the cost of the inhabitants; he gets about sixpence per annum from each house and a handful of food daily; he has his privileges and his annual corn at the time of harvest; he is not refused by any gardener when he asks for vegetables; he gets gifts of different kinds when there are festivals and pleasure days. A certain fee is allowed him when he shaves the hair of a firstborn child for the first time, and he also gets a cloth from the village bridegroom when he seeks the help of the barber to dress his hair and to shave his face just before his wedding. The village barber has no fixed place where he can take people for shaving; he is at the beck and call of anybody. He receives his customers or patients under the shade of a tree, or on the bank of a pool or a tank or at a stable, or in the veranda of a house.

The barber will go to the corner of the backyard of a house and there sit down conveniently with his customer. Then he begins to sharpen his razor on a small bone, finishing it off on a small piece of leather—this smooths the edge of the razor. He wets the head with water and rubs it well with his hand, and uses his razor at the spot he has rubbed, whether it be the head or the face. The Indian villagers do not wear beards as a rule, but the Mahomedans do. The barber has to make a clean shave of everything except the moustache. When a man submits himself to a barber he is cruelly tormented; some parts are sure to be bleeding; there are several cuts on his face and head; every inch shaved by the barber will have a burning sensation for hours together. When a man is being shaved he cries out '*Appa*' ('O father!') if he feels much pain; but the barber goes on shaving, though the man still shrinks, and utters '*Annada?*' ('What do you mean, fellow?'). Then the barber tries to sharpen the razor on the skin of his right leg or on the skin of his left hand. This is a very peculiar, and by no means successful, method of sharpening a knife. Then he applies it again, and if he still finds that his razor is but a handsaw he commences to tell his customer some stories of young girls of the village, and with these the man forgets for the time his pain. If he belongs to that class which requires a clean shave from head to foot he has to exercise his patience for an hour or two.

When the barber shaves the neck-hair some men are accustomed to try and please the barber by promising to give him a pair of new cloths on the next festival day, or a sheep or a fowl to be killed at the next New Year's Day. In this way they renew and multiply their promises without any intention of fulfilling them. The barber, too, takes his own turn and plays tricks. If he finds that a customer of his does not pay his annual allowance, or bestow his usual gifts, he dodges him by saying that he will come down to his house and shave him and his male children at a fixed time—on the 12th, Friday next; but he does not mean to go on that day. If the barber again be questioned he fixes another date, another, and yet another, till the man gets tired. Then the man brings a charge against the barber to the village court. The village 'Court of Arbitration' settles the dispute between the barber and the villager.

If a barber finds a worse customer in the village he determines to disgrace him. He goes straight to the house of his bad customer and calls him out to be shaved. Both the villager and the barber then go to the shade of a tree a little way from the village. There they sit down, and the barber begins to shave the man. While one side of the head is being shaved the barber offers an insult to the customer, which the man cannot bear. So he begins to abuse the barber, and a regular quarrel takes place. The barber uses only some indecent expressions, and takes care not to hurt the man. The villager, being a man of higher caste than the barber, cannot control his passion, and so he strikes the barber. That is exactly the thing that the barber wanted. He leaves the villager there *half-shaved* and takes up his belongings and runs off to the village court-house, where he lodges his complaint against the villager, whom he has left half-shaved. It is a great disgrace to be seen walking through the village half-shaved, and it is a very strange spectacle in any nation. The poor villager covers his head with his upper cloth and goes home filled with sorrow and shame.

The *kuddymaken*, or the 'son of the village,' does not always keep himself to his profession. Sometimes he turns village surgeon. He has a peculiar lancet, and with this he performs his wonderful operations. If a villager happens to have some eruption upon him he seeks the aid of a barber. The manner in which he operates is altogether unscientific and troublesome. If he has to operate on a boil he cuts it in a cross form with his crude knife without any consideration of its fitness for opening. He does not know how to apply chloroform, but he puts the patient under the influence of alcoholic liquors. However clever he may think himself to be, his operation is neither more nor less than torturing and butchering; but we must bear in mind that his charges are next to nothing.

The village barbers are wonderful fellows for cock-fighting; they generally rear fighting cocks, often half a dozen of them.

The privilege of getting food from their neighbours enables them to feed these cocks. Some of them are very skilful in handling the fighting cocks when the lancets are attached to their feet. They smartly catch their own cock when he flies against his rival. The barbers who delight in cock-fighting will carry their cocks even to a distance of ten miles, and there they will spend a whole day—without having any noontide meal—till nine or ten at night. If the cocks are wounded in fighting the men are full of anxiety concerning them. They chew a bit of dry ginger and blow into the mouth, nostrils and ears of the wounded and fainting birds; they put a wet cloth on the head of the wounded creature and pour a few drops of water into its mouth in order to refresh it. If a barber happens to win with a bird it is a day of great joy and victory for him. When he approaches his village he sends for the parish drums, and to the deafening noise of these drums he marches through the dull streets of the village to his home. On the following day he runs down to the house of the goldsmith with a piece of silver, of which he wants a ring made to decorate the leg of his victorious bird.

We have said enough about the inefficiency of the barbers in shaving; but there is a story current which serves to show that there are honourable exceptions among them. It appears that a king happened to be on a visit to his country seat. While there, a barber was summoned to shave his face. When the barber arrived he found that the king was sleeping. He took courage, however, to approach the king, who was sleeping in the outer court of his country seat, and actually succeeded in shaving him without awaking him. Then the barber went away. When the king awoke he ordered his attendant to bring the barber in. The barber came in, and prostrated himself before the king, and informed his highness, with his body trembling, that he had already shaved him while he was sleeping. The king was highly pleased with his country barber, and loaded him with gifts.

The wives of barbers are nurses, and are useful in attending sick children. When children suffer from coughs or bronchitis the barber's wife knows a herb with which to treat them. Throat complaints are cured by these women, who insert some mixture with the help of their fingers. Although this application of the finger seems a cruel kind of treatment, it certainly relieves the pain of the children, and causes them to sleep well.

The barber's wife is also serviceable to the village Brahmin widows. She is called in by them twice a month or so in order that she may shave their heads.

She sometimes plays the part of the village fool by carrying messages to strange lovers, for which she is amply paid. Her services are very highly appreciated by profligate village women, to whom she is helpful in the carrying out of their unlawful schemes. The barber woman is also known as the midwife of the village. The mother of a barber, or a widowed sister of a barber, takes up this profession, but the midwife is too often an angel of death. She treats her patient with extreme inconsiderateness, and even with cruelty. Not having the slightest knowledge of medical science, or instruments with which to meet cases of difficulty, many lives are lost in consequence of her rough and unskilful treatment. Reform in relation to these family exigencies is urgently needed to save the lives of the women of India.

7. THE POTTER (*Kusavan*).

No Indian village could exist without the help of a potter. According to the classifications of India, the potter belongs to a subdivision of one of the classes in this land of caste. He wears a sacred thread in order to indicate that he belongs to the old Aryan stock, and he has a tuft of hair on the front part of his head, which distinguishes him from all other classes of the community, except a certain class of Brahmins in the Travancore country, and a certain class of people in Malabar. The term *kusavan* (a potter) is said to be derived from the Sanscrit word *ku*, signifying 'earth,' which is the material in which he works. *Avan* is a personal termination. There are 124,332 potters in Southern India itself.

The potter lives in a village which he finds suited to his calling, and this he makes his centre. He has a district of villages to which he supplies his pots. He is unlike the *dhoby* and the barber, for he does not get his wages from the villagers generally. He has a simple machine, which has remained unaltered for some two thousand years. He takes no trouble to improve his machinery or to lessen his manual labour. He and his family are the workers in his workshop. The material he works with is clay, and this he prepares at great cost of time and labour. He digs up the earth, and brings it home, and begins by straining it. Then he puts this earth in a corner of his yard, and pours water over it constantly. He and his wife spend hours together in treading this clay. Then he takes it, and puts it in a mill, which grinds it suitably for his purpose. According to the design he has in his mind, he takes up a certain quantity of clay, and forms it into a round ball, which he places on the top of his machine. This machine is made out of a few pieces of wood in the form of a wheel. He puts the wheel in motion, and when it revolves he touches the clay ball with a well-shaped small wooden piece on all sides of the ball to give the formation of the vessel which he wants to bring out.

The method and instruments with which he works are simple, but the skill that he displays in shaping the particular form of vessel he requires is very remarkable. After turning the vessel upon the wheel, he takes it into his hands, and touches it here and there with a piece of wood. When he finishes in this way a certain number of vessels for cooking and other purposes, he exposes them to the sun to be dried. For this purpose the winter season is not suited. When the vessels are dried they are kept in a hole and covered up with stubble, dry cow-dung and straw. When the vessels are burnt in a kiln, they are left in it to be cooled during one day and one night. Then the potter brings them home. He separates the vessels according to the number of orders which he has received. He lays up all the pots, numbering twenty-five to thirty, in a nest made out of ropes. He carries a load himself, and engages others also to carry the loads, and walks to some distant village, where he supplies the goods that were ordered.

If the villagers are in a hurry for the vessels they go to his house to fetch them.

Among the different kinds of vessel which a potter makes are pots, small or large, for cooking food; hollow pans for making Indian curries or soups; flat pans to fry meat or Indian vegetables; waterpots of large and small size; tubs for watering the domestic animals; a number of pots, both large and small, in which to store up the provisions, and these are generally called *adduku panais* (studded pots in rows). This row of pots is used to secure the valuables; the

THE WELL.

small pots and vessels are used to carry the food of a farmer to the fields. The poor class of people use earthen articles for the purpose of eating and drinking. Besides these, the potter makes earthen rings for water wells, and small, movable jars to hold grain.

In the form of wages, the potter has a fixed measure of grain annually from every farmer to whom he supplies the necessary vessels twice in the year. If they want any vessel during the interval, they must pay the usual price for it. The labouring class should pay the price of every vessel which they purchase from him. In a wealthy farmer's house might be found about 300 vessels, large and small. In the house of a labourer there would be from ten to thirty vessels of the most necessary kinds. Some of the village officials get vessels forcibly from the poor potters by exercising an undue authority over them.

Whatever may be the usefulness of the potter, one thing is certain, he creates innumerable gods and goddesses for the villagers. And he also makes for them images of dogs, elephants, cows, tigers, horses, cocks and hens, children, men and women, of monstrous size and having a frightful appearance. These images are offered by the villagers at the demon temples.

The potters, as a class, are simple-minded, harmless folk. They will never face a man who tries to pick a quarrel with them. They, like other villagers, find no opportunity to educate their children. They move in a limited circle, and it is little wonder they do not care to improve themselves, for they have always to meddle with mud, and mud alone. To illustrate the simplicity of a potter, we may give here one instance. On a certain day, the village chief sent his peon to the village where the potter lived, and he was to bring certain vessels from the potter for nothing. Knowing of this, the potter went to a palm-grove, and hid himself there. The peon who passed by that way saw a man standing under a palm-tree. But the peon was not able to make out that he was the potter. So he simply asked him: 'Why are you standing there?' The man replied: 'I am looking at the palm-tree, and thinking whether I could make a plough for myself.' The peon then said: 'Ah! you are a *kusavan*' (a potter or a fool). 'Would anyone use a palm-tree for a plough? It is quite unusual.' Then said the potter: 'Ah! how could you know that I was here?' At once the peon knew that he was the village potter, to whom he was going, and caught him by the hand, and said: 'Lo, fellow! you have been hiding yourself under the palms. Now come on and give me the vessels.'

8. BRICKLAYERS (*Kuttars*).

There is no particular class of people who are called 'bricklayers.' The unfashionable and uninteresting buildings do not require skilful and well-trained bricklayers. However, there are bricklayers, who go about with their trowel and plumb-line in their hands. These men generally belong to the *vellala* class; they are known as *kuttars*. They are engaged to build houses for the upper and middle classes of villagers. The lower class of villagers do the work of raising the four walls of their own huts. Sun-burnt bricks, clay, and rough stones are the materials with which the village bricklayer works. He need not spend much time in planning to raise his buildings, for the village building is simple and plain. He has to raise, for a middle-class villager, a long hall, two rooms, and a kitchen, with the usual Indian veranda, called *pial.* To erect this building the bricklayer works for some months. The bricks are made and dried in fields before they are removed to the site of the buildings. Then the bricklayer engages a few boys and girls, who are called *sittals*, and also a few working-class women, to help him in his work.

One may see a village bricklayer using his plumb-line, in order to make the owner of the building think that he shows great ingenuity in making the walls upright. But in fact he only wastes his time, for the walls appear to the naked eye quite crooked. The head-bricklayer gets daily wages of eight annas, or eightpence. The minor workers get threepence per day, the women get fourpence. In some villages the woman is classified with a minor worker, and then she is paid only threepence per day. While raising the walls the bricklayer carefully avoids making openings for ventilation. He puts no side-windows in the walls. When the time comes to put the door-posts into position, the bricklayer gets drunk, and makes himself merry at the expense of the owner of the house. If the owner of the house is a man of means, he makes the day one of great rejoicing to all his workers.

He offers a blood sacrifice of a lamb at the door-post, and breaks cocoanuts, and burns incense, and thus he invokes the blessing of his family god, in order to prevent the house from falling, and to get him to stand at the door-post, so as to prevent the angel of death from entering the house. He also paints the lintel with a red paste, as a sign of the blood sacrifice he has offered to his god. Possibly the Jewish sacrifice of the Passover, instituted by God, has found its way to these remote Indian villages, where it is still practised in different forms. After this ceremony the roofing of the building takes place. Almost all the Indian houses have thatched roofs, and this is a cause of great calamities, and even loss of life and property, in the rural parts of India, because fire breaks out so readily in them.

When the building of a house is finished, the bricklayer is rewarded by the owner with a pair of new cloths and a turban. The owner also invites his friends and relations, and feeds them with a sumptuous meal at the opening of the house. In some cases he also gives alms to the poor of the village. He is bound to invite his family priest to perform the ceremonies on an auspicious day. He sends some of his relations to the nearest town to procure plantain, plantain-leaves, cocoanuts, and vegetables of all kinds. And thus he collects some of the necessary things which he could not procure in the village. Very early in the morning of the opening day he and the members of his family go to a tank, or well, and there they finish their bathing and their *pujahs* before the sun rises. At a fixed hour the family priest comes to the house to perform the ceremonies. He kindles a holy fire in the middle of the house, and places a lamp, two earthen pots filled with holy water, several measures of rice, heaped on plantain-leaves, with plantains, vegetables, and flowers, nicely arranged. Before these offerings sit the family, the priest, and his companions, and he utters prayers for about an hour. Then he blesses the owner of the house and his family, and sprinkles the urine of a cow all over the building. Then he blesses the ovens and fireplaces, in which the lady of the house places an earthen pot, boils milk and cooks food for herself and family and invited guests. Immediately the female members and female friends commence the cooking for the day. Of course, some of the male members also take part in this. The family priest bundles up the rice, fruits, vegetables, and other offerings, and carries them off to his home to enjoy them. The village bricklayer also puts in an appearance on this occasion, and makes himself quite at home.

Of late it has become the fashion for well-to-do classes to build stone houses, in order to save their dwellings from the danger of fire, and to protect themselves from the strong and merciless hands of the burglars. In these the bricklayer has displayed his skill by placing a few artificial peacocks and other shapes of animals in different parts of the house. There are some houses having upper stories built by the bricklayer, but these are used as storehouses for different kinds of grain, and they are only suited for such a purpose.

9. THE WELL-DIGGERS (*Ottars*).

These people are natives of Otlyam, a country north of Madras. The term 'Oddan' seems to be a corruption of 'Odhra' (modern, 'Orissa'). There are 172,202 *ottars* in South India. The eldest members of the caste officiate as priests. Their marriage ceremony is brief and very inexpensive. While the bridegroom ties a *thaly* to the bride's neck, the relatives present throw some rice mixed with turmeric on the heads of the bridal pair. Widow marriages are both permitted and practised. They drink alcoholic drinks freely; even their women and children partake of this tempting cup. In relation to the rite of marriage, these people have little or no principle, hence polygamy and divorces are very common among them. A man is freely allowed to marry any number of wives and to discharge them at his pleasure, but the woman is strictly restricted from changing partners after having had eighteen husbands already. They favour a woman who has divorced six husbands, and is married to a seventh man; the blessing of such a woman on a bridal pair is greatly prized.

The *ottars* spend all their days in digging the earth. The wells which supply pure and fresh water to villagers, the reservoirs which quench the thirst of cattle and provide opportunity for the ablutions of villagers, the channels which carry the river waters into the bosom of the country to supply the tanks, are all dug by the *ottars*. They are a very active and energetic people, born to die as diggers of the earth. Their coarse baskets, rough spades, long crow-bars, and country pickaxes, are property handed down from generation to generation.

These men are scattered throughout the length and breadth of India. They pitch their movable huts wherever they can find work. Men dig the earth with their spades or pickaxes, and the women do the work of carrying it in their baskets. They get their wages according to the amount of work that is executed. As both sexes labour hard they are healthy and strong in physique, simple and harmless in mind, and very temperate in their habits. There is sufficient evidence to prove that this class of people were once very serviceable to ancient kings and princes as sappers and miners.

There are two classes of *ottars*, the *mun ottars* (earth diggers) and the *kullottars* (stone-cutters). They monopolize all the earth-diggings of the villagers, who treat them very kindly, and advance them money with confidence. The landowners who have extensive tracts of lands engage these earth-diggers to make their lands fit for cultivation, to deepen their tanks, to raise their banks, and to open new channels.

THE WELL.

They work willingly and patiently from morning to sunset, taking only an hour for their noontide meal. Their principal articles of food are raggee and different kinds of rats. In India there are more than eighteen different kinds of rats. The *ottar* can choose any one of these eighteen kinds of rats for his dinner. The wife, on returning from work, prepares the meal out of raggee flour and makes some fine rat-soup. When the man returns home he bathes in cold water, and then relishes the dish which has been prepared by his wife, and takes for his drink water. There is hardly a more hard-working man in India than the *ottar*, and he enjoys sound health, and finds himself quite equal to his work. The rough ways are smoothed, and the crooked paths are made straight by these *ottars*. They are also remarkable for their cleanliness.

A very interesting story is current that the god Siva once assumed the form of an *ottan*. Near the famous Madura city, which is situated on the bank of the Vyga, a holy river, which had descended from heaven, was at a certain time overflowing. By the furious force of the current a large breach was made on the bank of the river, and this involved extreme danger for the magnificent city. Being alarmed at this threatened breach, the king Pandyan summoned a man from every house in the city. The king himself headed the band, and they set to work to repair the breach. There was a widow in the city who was earning her livelihood by selling *puddu* (rice-pudding). The peons who were collecting men for the work of repairing the breach went to this widow, and demanded a man from her house. The woman being a child-widow, and not having any male member in her family, was unable to obey the order of the king. However, she saw a young man by her side, and said to him, 'Go and do the work for me, and I will feed you this day with my *puddu*.'

This she said without knowing that he was the incarnated Siva. The young man readily consented, and followed the peon to the breach. The task-masters numbered the men according to the number of the houses, and found them all correct. While the band was busily engaged in the work, the young man who represented the widow was dodging about here and there, and presently he went to the widow and asked for some pudding. The woman willingly gave him some *puddu*, and hurried him to the bank. But the young man was found by the taskmasters to be lazy and inactive, and he often absented himself from the work. He was warned to stick to his business, but all in vain. It was nearly the time for the king to come on a visit of inspection, and everyone was doing his best, but this young man was between the pudding and the river water. This they brought to the notice of the king, who, being provoked in anger, struck the young man. At once the young man disappeared, and the stroke was felt by all the people of the city, as if it had been struck on the back of each one of them. The queen in the palace, the poor widow at her eating-house, and the king himself felt it. By this the king, the peons, the taskmasters, and the poor widow all knew that the young man who had played the part of an *ottan* was none else than the god Siva, who had come to help the poor widow in her time of need.

10. THE STONEMASON.

The village stone-cutter belongs to the group of five artizans of the village. He generally lives where there is solid rock which will suit his purposes. He opens his workshop under the burning sun on the open rock. He has a few chisels of different kinds and some iron hammers. With these simple tools he turns out some really good and useful work. He makes the stone for grinding curry materials; the mortar in which to pound rice; and the mills — which are primitive in style — for grinding the flour. He can also make stone steps, pillars, beams, doorposts, jars, stands, troughs for watering the cattle, and other useful articles that are required for domestic use. He is not a monthly or annually paid artizan, but he receives suitable payment from the people for all the articles with which he supplies them. He does not go about to collect grain and vegetables from the villagers. If any villager chooses to give him a gift in the form of grain or fruit, of course he is only too happy to accept it.

The skill of the famous Indian stonemasons has been displayed in the erection of the temples of India. The remarkable way in which groups of animals and human figures are carved out of the solid rock in some of the most famous ancient Hindu temples, speaks volumes for the skilfulness of the Indian stonemason. There is a temple (consecrated to the Hindu god Subrawanian, the second son of the god Siva) at Kalugumalai, in the Tinnevelly district of Southern India, which is noted for its singular situation under a solid rock. The cave itself is well worth a visit, and the carvings in solid rock are simply marvellous.

In the temple of Sirramgam, in the Trichinopoly district, there are several indications of the skill of the stonemason. There are many beautiful pagodas, which shoot up into the sky to a lofty height, in the midst of hundreds of palm-trees and mango-trees, between the two great rivers, the Kavery and the Kolliram. The beautiful and attractive stone pillars, which stand in some of the temple *mandapam* (cloisters) were first conceived in the mind of the stonemason, and then fashioned into shape by his skilful hands. At the bottom of the pillar is the figure of a bear ten feet in height; in the middle of the pillar is a horse about eight feet in height; on the back of the horse there is a hero holding a long spear in his right hand, which is passing through the bear that holds up the pillar. On the top of the pedestal there hang different kinds of Indian fruits. There are several pillars of this kind, and they differ only in the forms given to the animals.

The stonecutters also make innumerable gods and goddesses for the people. They make gods with human bodies and animal heads, or with animal bodies and human heads. Their fingers have formed images of all the living creatures of India, and placed them in the sacred buildings of the Hindu community.

It is a general complaint that the ancient Indians did not leave any proper record of the history of their land. The stonecutters have to some extent made up for this deficiency. They have told the histories and mysteries in the works of their hands. The inscriptions carved by them in various temples some two to three thousand years ago are still read with interest, and they are often used in deciding the disputes as to the rights of the peasants, the priests, and the princes of the land.

There are many stories connected with the scientific knowledge of the stonemasons. There is a beautiful and even magnificent temple in the historical and ancient city of Madura. This temple was built by the founders of the Pandyan Dynasty, and afterwards much improved by Terumal Naick, the latest Hindu ruler of Madura. In this temple there is a *royer gopuram* (the great pagoda), which was built by Terumal Naick. There are two large stone pillars in this *royer gopuram.* A certain stonemason, by order of the king, brought the stones from the mountain, and placed them in the pagoda, and then died. His son came, and attempted to follow in the footsteps of his father in erecting the royal monument to the goddess Meenatchi, and then he died. By-and-by his son came to the temple to pay his vows. As he entered the *royer gopuram* he saw the great stone pillars. As he looked at them he thought that his grandfather had made a mistake in bringing one of the stones and placing it in the sacred place, and he gave expression to his feelings while he was standing in the temple, saying that the temple was polluted according to 'building science,' inasmuch as in one of the two huge pillars a frog was still alive at a certain spot towards the top of the pillar. This statement was brought to the notice of the king, and the man was summoned at once into his presence. The king asked the stonemason, 'Have you said that my temple is polluted on account of one of the pillars being placed in the main entrance of the temple?' 'Yes, your highness,' politely said the man. 'If you cannot prove your statement to be true, remember your head will be severed from your body,' said the king in a very severe tone of voice. Having placed his life as the pledge for the truth of his statement, the stonemason boldly asked the king to follow him to the temple. The king and his courtiers went. The stonemason requested one of the servants of the king to place a ladder beside the pillar, and to go up to the top, and break off a certain portion of the pillar with a hammer. When several small pieces had been broken off a stone frog actually fell down, to the great surprise of the king and his advisers. The king immediately ordered his servants to bring gifts from the palace, and these he presented to the stonemason, and he even bestowed upon him royal honours.

11. THE BASKET-MAKERS (*Kuravars*).

The word *kuravars* means 'mountaineers.' Since the men from the mountain districts have come into the fertile plains they have taken to the occupations of fortune-telling, bird-catching, and basket-making. Some of the men and women are inveterate robbers; the eyes of the public are kept on them. Their pilfering habits prevent their moving freely among the other tribes, so they have to lead a secluded life. When the villagers would do business with them they bring them into the front yards of their houses, settle matters there, and then quickly send them away.

On some of the large Hindu temple festivals thousands of people come from all parts of the country to pay their vows and to worship. These large masses of people are obliged to spend their days and nights under the trees, in the open fields, and in temporary sheds. There is, of course, great confusion and uproar with the noise of the devotees, the merrymakers, the pleasure-seekers, and the buyers and sellers. At such scenes the *kuravars* find a fine opportunity for exercising their pilfering skill. Here a woman cries out that her earring is gone; there a man cries out that his handkerchief, with some money in it, is lost; here a lad is crying out that his upper-cloth is lost; there a girl is complaining that her finger-rings are missing. Everyone will be sure to suspect the *kuravars*, who are stealthily moving about. Constantly *kurava* men and women are being caught, examined, and illtreated by the police officers.

During the time of harvest the *kurava* women are scattered abroad in the villages, with their funny baskets and their curious cane, trying to tell fortunes. They go to every house, especially when the men are out, and find fine opportunities for deceiving the ignorant women. The fortune-teller will catch hold of a young unmarried woman or her mother and will tell her all sorts of things about her future husband, the direction from which he will come, and his wealth and beauty. Sometimes she will also fix the time of marriage for the waiting young woman. This naturally pleases the inmates of the house, who are glad to give some measures of grain to the fortune-teller, and in this way she goes on from house to house receiving grain for her support.

Some of these people are engaged in making baskets, which are made from palm-leaves and the branches of other trees. The men, women, and children are engaged in making them for several days together. They make baskets for the use of those who sow grain, for carrying the grain, for removing cow-dung, for the use of the rice and grain in the house. These baskets are taken in large numbers to the general market (*Sandy*), which is held once a week in some central village, to which people gather from the villages around. Having sold their baskets, the *kuravars* purchase grain with their money and take it to their homes.

They dwell in small huts. They make free use of arrack and toddy in all their ceremonies, and even on ordinary occasions they indulge somewhat freely in alcoholic drinks.

They are, like some other aboriginal tribes, devil-worshippers, and social morality is no concern of theirs. Their elders often hold a court of divorce in order to settle disputes between the husbands and wives of the clan.

The customs connected with the settlement of disputes between a husband and a wife are exceedingly curious. If a basket-maker has a charge to bring against his wife he must call a court of divorce. This court consists of about a dozen elders of the tribe. The man who makes the charge must summon these elders; he himself must go to every village and inform each elder of the nature of the charge which he is preferring against his wife. When all the parties are informed they fix a day on which the court is to sit. The sitting of the court commences about eight o'clock in the morning, under a tree outside a village. The judges, having partaken of their morning meal, sit on the ground facing one another, but leaving a sufficient space in the centre. The two parties with their witnesses must wait at a sufficient distance to be out of hearing. The man who brings the charge must provide a big jar full of arrack and place it in the centre of the group; then he must prostrate himself before the elders. In some cases he is required to place one or two roast fowls with the arrack. The plaintiff must also take special care to bring a *ullakku* (one-fourth of an Indian measure) or a few cocoanut-shells. The judges divide themselves into two parties, one taking the part of the plaintiff and the other the part of the accused. The chief judge fills the measure with arrack and drinks, then he asks the plaintiff to state the charge which he brings against his wife before all the judges. As soon as the suit is heard the chief judge fills the cup with the liquor and passes it to the judge next to him, addressing the plaintiff with the words 'Well done.' Now the cup goes around, and each judge gets a drink; the cup goes round once again, and then the judges begin to get excited and proceed to argue out the case very elaborately. Suddenly one of them will stop the proceedings of the court by asking the judges to have a drink.

The cup then goes round again. Perhaps one of the judges will then throw a new light on the case, which will greatly add to the confusion and excitement. The accused is not yet brought in to give her statement, but the jar full of liquor is consumed by the judges and they become drunken to a helpless degree, so that they have to postpone the case until some future time. The judges then disperse without even taking leave of each other. The poor plaintiff now must wait until he can find money enough to purchase another jarful of liquor. When he manages to get that the judges assemble again, under the same tree, and behave in precisely the same manner. In this way it may take years for a man to get a divorcement from his wife in the court of the *kuravar* judges. If a woman prefers a case against her husband she must go through the same routine. Hence the proverb, 'Appadi sol valakki aven keyel kodu olakki,' *i.e.*, 'Say so the case and give the cup in the company's hand.'

The marriage customs of this caste are also peculiar —each party endeavours to ascertain the mind of the other party privately. Having ascertained it, they consult a Brahmin about the intended marriage. If he gives a favourable answer the bridegroom's party proceeds to the bride's house to arrange for the marriage. They take arrack with them and give it to the bride's father. He also procures arrack, and both parties drink freely of it, distribute the betel, and then begin to settle the conditions of the marriage. The bridegroom's father asks the bride's father whether he intends to give his daughter in marriage to his son. If he replies in the affirmative the bridegroom's father gives him a little arrack in a cocoanut-shell and also a piece of tobacco. This is called 'the arrack and tobacco of confirmation'; also a *jembu* full of water is placed before the couple, and a grass named *thurbai* (*i.e.*, *Agrestis linearis*) is put into the water. This is regarded as an oath between the couple.

A feast then follows, with arrack and toddy. The parties again meet after dinner to settle the *parisam* or nuptial present, which, if the bride be related to the bridegroom, is four *narungus*. One *narungu* is equal to rupees 8 3-4. Of these one is paid immediately, together with rupees 1 3-4, which are spent in feasting. The other three *narungus* are paid at the rate of one per annum.

But if the bride be not related to the bridegroom, the *parisam* amounts to ten or twelve *narungus*, out of which four are to be paid immediately, together with rupees 1 3-4 for the feast, and the remainder is to be paid within five years. If these sums are not paid regularly, the bride should be sent away to her father's house.

In cases where separation occurs, the sum given as the nuptial present should be returned, and anyone willing to pay the same amount may take the woman again in marriage.

On the *mukurtham*, or marriage-day, a *pandal* is constructed in the bride's house. The bridegroom shaves himself, bathes, and is dressed in new clothes. Having drunk some arrack, the bridegroom starts for the bride's house, with garlands on his neck, attended by his relations and friends. The bridegroom's sister goes to the room where the bride is, dresses her with new clothes, puts garlands on her neck, and ties on the *thallei*, and the couple are then regarded as married.

The bride and the bridegroom sit under the *pandal*, facing the east, and a piece of timber is covered with a clean cloth. The bride's father takes the right hand of his daughter, and places it in the right hand of the bridegroom, who holds it. Then they both stand up, holding each other's hands, and, having walked round the *manavarai* three times, retire to a room, where they are seated looking eastwards. Then follows a feast of arrack. The next morning the bridegroom and bride, with their relations and friends, start for the bridegroom's house.

In this caste children are promised in marriage even before their birth. Two men, who wish to have a marriage between their children, will say one to the other, 'If your wife should have a girl and mine a boy, or yours a boy and mine a girl, they must marry.' And to bind themselves to this pledge, they exchange tobacco, and the bridegroom's father makes a feast of arrack or toddy to the coming bride's relations. But if, after the children are grown up, the Brahmin should pronounce the omens unpropitious, the marriage is not consummated, and the bride's father pays the cost of the arrack and other spirits that were used at the betrothal.

12. THE OIL-PRESSERS (*Vaniars*).

The oil-pressers form a very distinct class, and they have a priest of their own caste. They do not live in every village, but they choose a central village, so that they may have easy access to other villages. They wear a sacred thread, and they belong to the Siva sect. They are flesh-eaters and total abstainers. They marry their daughters very early, and their widows do not re-marry. They are a quiet and inoffensive people. There are 151,919 oil-pressers in Southern India.

Their oil-mill is called *chekkoo*, and it is made out of the trunk of a large tree. This mill is still in its primitive state (see illustration). The forefathers of the oil-pressers introduced this mill for pressing oil some two thousand years ago, and no improvement of any kind has been made in it. The mill is usually worked by two bullocks, but some can be worked by a single bullock. Some of the mills are therefore known as 'double bullock oil-presses,' and others as 'single bullock oil-presses.'

The oil-pressers buy their own oil seeds, such as gingelly, lamp-oil, cocoanut, *pinaykai*, and *ilippay* seeds, and they sell the oil to the villagers. The oil-pressers generally carry the oil in earthen vessels. The villagers buy the gingelly oil, and rub it on themselves from head to foot, either on Saturdays or on Wednesdays, and then wash it off with *seeyakkay* or *poonack*, the Indian soap. They also use it in preparing their curries (sauces) and cakes and sweets. For these purposes cocoanut-oil is used in some parts of India. The other oils are used for burning in the lamps.

There is a characteristic Indian story connected with these oil-pressers. A certain oilmonger went to a village to sell oil. While he was on his way he began to aspire to something higher than his lot. He had heard of the beauty and accomplishments of the king's daughter, in the country in which he lived. He had indeed seen her himself on several occasions when she was driving with her father. So the idea came into his mind that he would like to marry the king's daughter, and if he did not he would die a bachelor. With this resolve in his mind, he was walking along, meditating upon the advantages that he would gain by marrying her. He thought that if he married a princess he would be highly respected by the people, and everyone would raise both hands over the head, and salute him whenever he came out of the palace. Then he thought that it was his duty to return the salute. So he abruptly let go the

THE OIL-PRESSER.

hands with which he was holding the oil-vessel, in order to lift them in returning the salute, and, of course, the oil-vessel fell down from his head, and broke to pieces, and the oil was lost. Now the poor fellow began to realize his position, and he thought he had made a mistake; but it was too late. As the loss was a serious one to him, he sat down by the wayside and began to cry and abuse his gods for bringing this misfortune on him.

Just at that moment a certain king's son with his followers happened to be passing that way, and he saw the poor man crying bitterly by the wayside. Having compassion on him, the prince sent one of his followers to find out what was the matter with him. When the prince's follower went to the oilmonger, he told him that he had lost his oil and oil-vessel, and all through his ambitious imaginations. The prince's followers took him to the prince, and made him relate his own story. When the oilmonger told the prince that he was thinking of marrying a certain king's daughter, this prince laughed at the idea. But he ordered the oil-monger to follow him to the nearest village. There he ordered him to be shaved and bathed, and then he gave him his own royal robes to put on, and made him ride in his palanquin, the prince disguising himself as an ordinary companion, and giving strict orders to all his men not to reveal the trick, but to address the oilmonger as if he were indeed the prince of Manianagar. He ordered them also to tell everyone whom they might meet on their way that this prince was an athletic champion and a great teacher of Vedanta philosophy, and a master of Hindu literature. Besides this, they must show him the most profound respect, and never reveal the fact that he was only an oilmonger whom they had picked up on their way. The prince himself played the part of a chief attendant. All of them entered the town in which the famous princess dwelt. The name of this princess was Panchaletchmi, which means, 'The possessor of beauty, wealth, courage, virtue and wisdom.'

As soon as they entered into the royal palace, they sent word to the king that Prince Kampeeran of Manianagar had come to marry the princess of Allagapuri, his famous daughter. The king, having heard the news, jumped for joy, for he had been waiting for several years to find a suitable husband for his daughter, who was the gem of his family. He at once ordered his courtiers to attend to the comforts of the prince and his companions. The prince of Manianagar and his followers were lodged in a separate palace, and there they were entertained according to the Oriental custom.

On the following day the princess of Allagapuri sent her maidens to see the new prince, and get some information about him from his followers. As soon as the maidens entered into the palace, the chief attendant received them courteously and treated them kindly. Some of the maidens were intelligent and well educated. When they saw the manners and the attainments of the chief attendant, they were struck with wonder. 'What need is there for us to see the prince? We have seen the chief attendant's manners, attainments and beauty; how much more wonderful must the prince be!' said these clever maidens among themselves.

However, one of them said, 'Let us go and stand at a distance, and see the prince before we return to our palace.'

So the chief attendant gave them a chance of just seeing the prince at a distance, and then sent them away. The maidens, having returned to the palace of the princess of Allagapuri, reported very flatteringly concerning the prince and his courtiers—so much so, indeed, that the princess made up her mind to marry him.

The king of Allagapuri sent several of his wise men to see the prince, and they were all met by the chief attendant, who answered every question that was put to him in relation to philosophy and literature to their entire satisfaction. They also returned with similar impressions to the maidens, and reported to the king, who was highly pleased, and made all arrangements for the marriage.

A certain auspicious day was fixed, and grand preparations were made, and at last the marriage was over. No sooner did the prince enter into the princess's palace than his chief attendant and his followers dispersed one by one.

There was a full moon when the marriage took place, and so the newly-married couple went up to the upper chamber of the palace on the full moon night. They walked on the terrace, looking at the sky, and the princess explained several things about the stars to the prince, who had been warned privately by the chief attendant to keep quite silent for a few days after the marriage. However, the poor husband could not control his tongue. He began to talk on the very day of his marriage, and, pointing to the full moon, he said, 'Ah, how nice the moon is! I like it. If I were in my home, I could press fifty measures of gingelly seed in my mill in this moonlight, and extract the oil before the sun rises.'

At once the heart of Panchaletchmi was broken, and she fainted and dropped down. Then the maidens came to her help, and conducted her to her bed. When she had recovered herself, she called her husband, and asked him to tell her the truth about himself, fearing that he must be an oilmonger in caste. She, being satisfied with his statement, then requested him not to reveal this to anyone, and she made him truly a wise man in her father's kingdom.

13. THE SWEEPER (*Toty*).

The village *toty* or sweeper is a menial servant of the village, and is under the direct control of the watchman. He sweeps the common places of the village, feeds the cattle in pounds, takes invitations or letters to the village officers, carries accounts, etc., to the district officer, and helps at the time of collecting the taxes from the ryots. He gets nominal pay from the Government. In addition to this, the villagers themselves give him a small annual grant. The sweeper is always taken from the out-caste classes of South India, so he cannot enter into any of the houses of the villagers.

If he feels thirsty while he is working in the hot summer days, he cries out for some water as he stands outside the house, or at a distance from the public well. Then someone who has compassion, either from the house or from the well, will pour water into his hands. The village sweeper is the poorly-paid menial of the village. What he gets from the Government and from the villagers is hardly sufficient to maintain himself and his family. Yet he is an energetic and hard-working fellow, and ever ready to obey the orders of the village officers.

If any district officers or *zamindars* happen to pass through the villages where there is no railway communication, the village officers receive an order from them to keep post bulls ready to draw their conveyances. As soon as the order is received, the village *toty* is summoned at once, whether it be night or day.

'Take the bulls, run up to that place (which may be about fifteen miles off), and wait till the master comes; when he arrives, hand over the bulls to his cart-men, and also these fowls,' says the village *munsiff* in an authoritative tone.

'I have not taken my *gangee* (*i.e.*, meal), sir,' says the *toty*.

'What do we care about that, you fellow! Go at once; run quick! carry a bundle of straw on your head for the bullocks,' says the village *munsiff*.

'I have only just returned from the *Taluga* Office, where master sent me with the letter; my wife is boiling some rice for me. Permit me to eat it and go, sir,' says the *toty*.

'Watchman, beat the beggar for his impertinence,' says the village judge. While this is going on, some kind-hearted villager turns up and intercedes with the judge on behalf of the *toty*, begging him to let the poor fellow take his meal before he starts with the pair of post bullocks. These usually belong to some villager, and are taken by force to serve the authority.

When the task is over the *toty* comes back to his officer, who orders him to go and watch his field, to keep the cattle out, and to drive away the wild beasts. In the villages near the mountains the *toties* are often wounded, and even killed, while they are attending to their duties. On the whole the *toties* are not treated with consideration by the village officers, and they are very ill-paid, but they are a patient and hard-working class.

14. THE FARMER (*Samusary*).

Farming in India is still in its primitive state. No scientific modes of operating on the soil have yet been introduced. As most of the villagers are ignorant, they are unable to form any idea of the art of tilling. Still, the farmer does his best in ploughing, weeding, sowing, reaping, and threshing. He keeps to the old style of his forefathers in all his operations. He never fails to manure the ground with cow-dung and goat-dung in order to enrich the soil. In the case of wet cultivation he brings an enormous quantity of different kinds of plants and scatters them over the fields; in order to take away the salt from them, and to help the plants to grow richer. Farming in India is quite unlike that in the Western world. To begin with, the farmer himself does not live in the midst of his fields. He lives in a village two or three miles distant from the ground which he is cultivating. His farm labourers, generally poor out-caste people, live in a settlement of their own about half a mile distant from the farmer's village. A wealthy farmer has about 200 acres of land, all freehold; he pays the annual tax of about four shillings per acre for dry land; and for the wet cultivation, when he grows rice, he has to pay from seven to twenty shillings per acre of land for one year. If the farmer lives in *zamindar* villages, he has to give 50 per cent. of the grain at the time of harvest (*zamindar* land is like the estates of dukes and lords in Europe).

There is a farmer in a village called Kylasapuram, who is a Reddy by caste. He has a large house built with mud walls in a square form, and having a thatched roof. At the entrance of his house he has two large *pials*, one on each side, which are intended for guests. On these *pials* several palm-leaf mats are kept ready, but the guest must be contented with the artificial pillows made of earth. The mat and this pillow make a comfortable bed for anyone who visits this farmer's house. In a corner of one of these *pials* there is a small room in which the farmer makes his daily *pujah* (prayers). In the inner circle of the house there are several rooms for keeping valuables in. At one corner of the house there are granaries, which are peculiarly built of small branches of trees and plastered with mud. This part has a thatched roof, and a small entrance provided with a lock and key. When anyone enters one of these granaries he is nearly suffocated for want of air, but the farm labourer, having opened the entrance awhile, is able to enter the granary, and even to remain there for an hour. Some of them sing songs of joy while they are removing the grain from the granary. By the side of these granaries there is a cattle-shed, in which are kept the milking-cows and buffaloes. There is no farmer in India without several milking buffaloes and also a few cows for his own domestic use. In some other part of his spacious house there are stone troughs for watering his cattle. He has a separate kitchen-house built in Oriental style, and fitted with hundreds of earthen vessels for cooking, and for keeping water for himself and his servants. The female members of the family and several males will be busily engaged in the kitchen preparing food for the family and for the farm labourers. There is also a neatly-built house in one corner of this farmer's yard, which is utilized as the private apartments. On another side of the house there is a shed for the bullocks which draw the *bandies* (carts). The farmer also has a large cattle-shed outside the house in an enclosure. There he has some forty or fifty bullocks kept ready for ploughing-work. In this building there are one or two large rooms in which he keeps the cotton-seeds for feeding the bullocks. He has also two separate sheds, one for the buffaloes and another for the cows who are not yielding milk. Besides these, he has temporary enclosures in the fields, some for his sheep, and others for his goats. This farmer has 500 sheep and about 700 goats. Outside of his village he has several large stacks of straw for his cattle. To manage all this business he has a head man, known as *pannai karan*, but the farmer and other members of his family are also actively engaged. There is no confusion in attending to their duties by any of the farm servants. There are about twenty men who are allowed to go in and out of the farmer's house to carry on the daily routine. Besides these men, there is quite a number of supplementary farm labourers. The men who have the privilege of moving in and out of the house are usually of the farmer's own caste. These men divide the daily work among themselves, and some of them have fixed work to attend to. For instance, four or five men come about four o'clock in the morning to remove the cow-dung, to prepare the cotton-seed, to dress the straw, and to attend to other matters which the farmer directs them to do. In fact, some of the labourers by turns sleep in the farmer's house. Some of the labourers carry the noontide meal from the farmer's house to the labourers who are working in the fields. On high days and holidays all the labourers are fed in the farmer's house with a grand meal. The farmer himself gets up from his bed at about four o'clock, and directs his men to attend to their duties. If it is the time of sowing, he goes himself to the field, and stays there for some hours. If it is the time of weeding, he visits several fields every day. There are different gangs of labourers engaged in weeding, and each group has a reliable head, who supervises their work. Harvest is the busiest and most pleasant time with the farmer and his labourers.

In a farmer's house there is paddy, raggi, millet, and different kinds of pulse, which have been grown in his own fields. These he utilizes for the family food. He has also poultry and sheep from which to make the dishes. These consist of some kind of sauces with fried meat. He has his milk, which he makes into curds and buttermilk and *ghee* (melted butter). He grows different kinds of Indian vegetables, chillies, coriander, and other things, which form the chief ingredients in preparing the curry. A village farmer can justly boast that what he gets from his field and farm is sufficient for his household except salt, saffron, pepper, and one or two other things which he is obliged to buy from a bazaar. A guest who goes to this farmer's house finds plenty to eat.

In Indian villages the farming is done by different classes of the people. Nowadays almost all the classes of the innumerable Indian castes have settled themselves down as peaceable cultivators of the soil; but the large portion of the most enterprising farmers are Vellalors, Reddys, and Naickers. All these three classes are known as the best village cultivators. A few of their social customs will be interesting to the reader.

The following is a description of the marriage ceremony among the Vellalors. 'When a young man is of an age to be married, his parents and relations begin to talk about girls who live both far and near. When they are satisfied about the parentage and appearance and possessions of a certain girl, the first thing they do is to go to the bride's house, and ask the parents of the bride for her *sathagam* (horoscope), which they examine carefully. Likewise the bride's relations examine the bridegroom's horoscope. If both horoscopes agree in the eleven essential points, the parties come to a settlement about the marriage. They invite an astrologer, and consult him as to an auspicious day. When the day is fixed, the bridegroom's nearest relations are invited to the bride's house, and they are provided with a good feast. The bride pays particular attention to the bridegroom's mother, and tries to win her affection and goodwill. After the meal a Brahmin comes to them, and to him several offerings are made in the form of fruits, rice, money, etc.; these are placed before him, and he is earnestly requested by both parties to foretell, by the practising of his art, how long the parties are likely to live a happy and pleasant life, and how many male and female children they will have. In part of one of the rooms a large square is formed of *chunnam* (lime-powder), in the south-western corner of which a brass lamp is placed, and near it some cocoanuts are broken, and plantains are placed upon one or two large plantain-leaves. This lamp is worshipped by all those who have gathered together. The bride bathes, and puts on the new cloth brought by the bridegroom's relations; and then, well adorned with flowers and ornaments, she is placed facing the east; the bridegroom's sister brings a basket containing three cocoanuts, three or nine plantains, some areca-nuts, and saffron. These presents are divided into three parts. One is given to the bride, which she returns to the bridegroom's sister, and the other two are given to the bride for her relations and friends. They then settle about the nuptial present, which, when agreed upon, is put into a piece of white cloth and given to the bride's father, who accepts it with great demonstrations of joy.

'Having received the certificate from the Brahmin priest, the parties go out in order to purchase necessary things for the wedding. It must be remembered that one of the causes of Indian poverty is the foolish way in which money is spent at marriages. If the parties are rich they spend a great deal. If their means are limited, they borrow to a fearful extent by mortgaging some of their property. Perhaps, if the bridegroom was the master of his house at the time of his marriage, he is afterwards burdened with the marriage debt. Soon after his marriage he becomes a care-stricken and miserable man. The poorer classes, when they are married, begin to live a most miserable life. They have to work hard day and night for their wages, and out of these they have to pay a portion regularly towards the marriage debt, often for several years.

'Now we turn back to the marriage party which we left purchasing the things required for the wedding feast. The first thing they buy is saffron. A quantity of rice is boiled in a new and coloured pot, and a cocoanut is broken near the bottom of the pot. Before giving gold to the goldsmith for ornaments for the bride, they ascertain a lucky hour and minute, and then take some sovereigns from the nuptial present and give them to him to be wrought into the required ornament. At a determined lucky minute they lay down the first brick in the south-west corner of the place appointed for the *manavarei* (a square daïs of earth erected in the centre of the *pandal*) and construct it. A branch from a fig-tree is set up in the south-west corner of the yard as a *mukurthakal* (or marriage post). Areca-nuts are first sent to the priest of the temple of Siva, and afterwards to all the relations. This serves as an invitation-card to the marriage. On the appointed night a good number of the bride's relations are sent to fetch the bridegroom, who comes in a palanquin to the bride's house with great pomp, and there he is joyfully received. When approaching the door some maidens wave their *alatthi* (lighted camphor) in token of respect; and on entering he is placed on a cot inside a room. Having partaken of milk and plantain—as it is supposed that he will be in need of some food—he comes out to the *manavarei*, and sits towards the east. A mango twig, to which are tied mango leaves dipped in saffron water, is placed in his hands, and this he takes to the south-western corner of the *pandal*, and there plants it. Then he enters another small room to have his face shaved by the barber.

'The bride is taken in a *palkee* to a tank, and there she bathes, with her maidens, and returns.

'Now commences the ceremony of tying on the *thali*. A Brahmin seats himself on a part of the *manavarei* facing the north, and before him a bright lamp burns; beneath this a *pilliar* (belly-god) is made out of cow-dung, and by the side of it are placed a measure of rice, some plantains, cocoanuts, and betelnuts.

'The adorned bridegroom receives sacred ashes from the Brahmin, and takes his seat on the other side of the *manavarei*, facing the east, with his young friends standing by him. The bridegroom's uncle (*i.e.* his mother's brother) sits by him, and receives his gifts. Afterwards the bridegroom is taken into a room, and the bride is adorned and brought to the *manavarei*, and seated upon it, facing the east. The bride's mother's brother, who sits by her, receives her gifts, and then retires with her from the *manavarei* into another room.

'After the bridegroom and the bride have retired to their respective rooms, the new cloths bought for them both are brought to the *manavarei* on two brass trays, and the Brahmin and other aged men there bless the cloths, and send them into the rooms.

'At the order of the Brahmin, the adorned bridegroom is

now brought back to the *manavarei*, and seated facing the east. The bride is also called for, and being adorned by her maidens with the new cloth, flowers, and jewels, she is taken into the kitchen, where there is a new pot. The bride draws three lines on it with saffron, and ties three betel leaves with a yellow string to its neck. The pot being placed on the fire, the bride pours into it a water-pot full of water, and goes to the *manavarei*. Here she sits on the bridegroom's right side.

'The bridegroom and the bride get down from the *manavarei*, and make a humble obeisance to the assembly, receive sacred ashes from them, and then go back to their respective places on the *manavarei*. The *thali* is put into a little wooden pot, and brought before the *guru* (priest), who blesses it himself and then gives it to the assembly for their blessing. They bless it and return it to the Brahmin.

'The barber keeps continually blowing the saugoo. A coloured pot is laid on an elephant (either real or earthen), the drums are beaten, and the trumpets are blown. The Brahmin pronounces some *mandiras* (prayers), and gives the *thali* to the bridegroom, who ties it slightly round the bride's neck; the bridegroom's sister, however, ties it tightly, and takes off one of the bridegroom's garlands, and puts it on the bride's neck. The bridegroom also takes one from his neck himself, and puts it on the bride's. The bride then takes one of hers and puts it on the bridegroom's. This is the end of the ceremony of tying the *thali*. The marriage is now complete, but there are still other ceremonies to be gone through.

'The Brahmin ties an iron ring and a bit of saffron to both of their hands. The bride's father then says to the bridegroom's father, "I have given my daughter in marriage to your son." The couple then unite their hands, and walk round the *manavarei* three times, tread upon the grinding-stone, look up in the sky at a star, and enter the room. Then the feast commences, and those who have come for the wedding make their money gifts to the bride's father.'

The Kammavar Naickers.—There is a most hard-working, persevering farming class known as *Kammavar Naickers.* These people have several village settlements of their own in India. They follow their forefathers' occupation in cultivating the soil. Every *Naicker* village has ten or fifteen landlords of the caste, each possessing several acres of land, several heads of cattle, and a large number of farm-labourers. To see an Indian model farmer one must go to this class. They cultivate all the different kinds of Indian grains and pulse in their fields; they also grow cotton in their alluvial and fertile soil, and this brings them in a large revenue.

Their women also work hard, both in the house and in the field. They are very simple in their mode of living, and exceedingly ignorant and superstitious.

These people belong to the Vishnu religious sect, but they worship all the gods and demons of India. They have some marked peculiarities. They are constantly spending large portions of their earnings in law-suits, and they are always ready to pick a quarrel. Their hard-earned money goes in this way to support the lawyers of the cities and towns.

If a man is married to a girl belonging to this caste he is taken to the bride's house and allowed to stay there for several months as a guest. If the bride's father is a rich man, the bridegroom is allowed to stay for a full year. During his stay in his father-in-law's house he is well entertained and fed. We have had the pleasure of seeing him soon after his marriage. It is simply marvellous to see how well this bridegroom fares. We give the entertainment provided for a single day.

At about seven o'clock in the morning the bridegroom gets a dozen large rice-cakes, about two dozen sweet cakes, two ounces of *ghee*, five ounces of sugar, and a dozen plantains. Our friend consumes all these, and a large *chembooful* of butter-milk. At about twelve o'clock half a measure of cooked rice, with different kinds of vegetables and a large quantity of pulse, four ounces of *ghee* with pepper-water, eight ounces of curds, sometimes one cooked fowl, three limes pickled, and a few other sauces are served. The young man patiently and steadily eats all these things up in about an hour's time. After this he takes his "forty winks.' At about three o'clock there comes before him a small basketful of sweet cakes, called *paniaram*, about five dozen plantains, some finger-cakes, a large quantity of Indian pudding, and about ten or fifteen twisted cakes, called *murookoo*. Having taken these eatables, this champion of eaters goes for an evening walk. At about 8 p.m. a meal similar to that served at noon again comes before him.

One of these bridegrooms, while he was staying at his rich father-in-law's house (he was a man with about 400 acres of land), at the time of the harvest, saw his father-in-law busily engaged with his men in cutting the stalks. On a certain day, while they were having a meal, the bridegroom asked his father-in-law, 'How many acres of land of stalks to be cut?' 'Several acres,' said the father-in-law. 'Well then, I shall be glad to be engaged in cutting the stalks from a hundred acres of land,' said the bridegroom. The following morning the bridegroom was taken by his father-in-law, and went to the field. Standing on an elevated ground, he pointed out with his finger the four boundaries of the acres of land in which the bridegroom had consented to work. The father-in law left the young man in the field, and went home. There is unbearable heat in the months of April and May in India, and, unfortunately, the task was undertaken in the month of April. No doubt there was a great deal of good intention in him. He commenced to cut the stalks for about fifteen minutes, but the heat was so severe that it melted his fat. His whole body began to perspire. The poor fellow became altogether exhausted. He was like a dog inhaling and exhaling the air; his breath became short, but he kept up his courage for awhile. At about 10 a.m. he returned home, having found himself quite unable to cut the stalks, even in a circumference of five yards.

In the house his father-in-law was giving out that his son-in-law had undertaken the task of cutting the stalks from a large part of his lands. As soon as he saw him return, he was anxious to know how he had got on in the field. The young man with shame replied that he was unable to cut the stalks to a distance of five yards, as the heat was so great and the day was burning hot. So he politely asked his father-in-law to set apart only ten acres of land for him, and to leave the rest for the other labourers to cut. On the following day the young man went at about eight o'clock in the morning, to the field, and remained there till nine, but found himself utterly useless even to cut the stalks for two yards. When he returned home at ten o'clock, he informed his father-in-law, with great reluctance, that the distance of ten acres of land was too great, and so he would like to have it reduced to four. The other parts of land must be given to other labourers. The father-in-law readily consented to the request of the young man, who went to the field in the forenoon, and was cutting the stalks when his father in-law came to him. The bridegroom took a stick, drew a line, and asked his ather-in-law to permit him to cut that part of the land only, and leave the rest to the farm-labourers. Late in the evening his father-in-law came to see him. By this time the young man was quite exhausted, and lying prostrated under a thorn-tree. He got up when he saw his father-in-law, and told him that he was unable to cut even the few yards which he had marked out, and so he begged his father-in-law to allow him to cut that distance of land which was marked out by turning his head round, practically the few stalks which stood under his foot. Hence arose the saying in this country—'Mappillay Naicker thattay aruthapol,' *i.e.*, 'As the bridegroom of the *Naicker* caste attempted to cut down the stalks.'

'The marriage customs of this caste keep them close to their occupation. The rule with this caste is, that the men shall marry the daughters of their sisters, *i.e.*, their nieces. Marriages are consequently made by persons between whom there exists a strange disparity of age. Oftentimes the bride is a mere infant, while the bridegroom is a full-grown man, and *vice versâ*. There is therefore no need to consult an astrologer in choosing a wife, though they do consult him in order to ascertain a lucky day for the wedding.

'On the day named by him the bridegroom's relations take with them a new cloth for the bride, a string of glass beads, the *parisam*, betel, saffron, sandalwood powder and flowers, and visit the bride's house, either on foot or in *bandies*.

'There they have a grand feast. This being over, the bride is directed to bathe, and afterwards she is taken to a room where they adorn her with flowers, saffron, and sandal-wood powder, tie the string of beads round her neck, and put on the new cloth which the bridegroom's relations have brought. They then serve out betel to the whole assembly. This they call "the betel of confirmation."

'Half the marriage is solemnized, they say, on this day. The amount of *parisam* given by the bridegroom's father is now placed in a *palkee* adorned with flowers and fragrant stuffs, carried round the village, and brought back. The bride's father takes the *parisam*.

'Both parties prepare the several articles required for the wedding; at a lucky minute they begin to boil the first pot of *paddy* in order to make rice. The *Múhúrtha Kal* is raised, and areca-nuts are sent to all the relations. A *pandal* is made, and the *manavarei* constructed under it.

'On the auspicious day for the wedding several of the bridegroom's friends and relations go to the bride's house to conduct her to the bridegroom's. The bride is adorned with costly ornaments, dress, and flowers, and taken round the village in a *palkee* in solemn procession, and thus brought to the bridegroom's house. A loud sound of drums and trumpets announces her arrival. A place is chosen contiguous to the dwelling-house, which is fenced round precisely in the same manner as a fold or pen for cattle, and the fence is high and strong; within this a temporary shed is erected, in which the Naicker and his bride are married, "in order to remind them that their fathers were without dwelling-places, tending their flocks in the fields." A pole is then erected, and upon it a few branches of the margosa-tree (*Melia azidarachta*) is tied, by the side of which the bridegroom stands. Some of his female relatives approach, and, dipping their forefinger in milk or oil, touch his forehead, shoulders and chest. After this a portion of rice is tossed over his head; he is then seized by a finger and led into the house.

'They next procure ten or fifteen earthen pots, which are ornamented with lines drawn with coloured chalks upon the outer surface, and place them in a convenient place, one over the other, the females of the house meanwhile chanting in Telúgú.

PLOUGHING.

'At the directions of the *guru*, the bridegroom retires to a room to adorn himself. The barber, having previously cleansed it with cow-dung, forms a *pillaiyar*, and, placing it in a corner, offers it a measure of rice, plantains, cocoanuts and betel. After performing these ceremonies he shaves the bridegroom's face and body, and washes him thoroughly, with the exception of the feet, the toe-nails of which are cut in the presence of the bridegroom's relations. The barber brings a cup of milk, with which he washes his feet, and then he cuts the nails. The milk which remains he carries round to the assembled guests, many of whom throw money into it.

'The carpenter prepares a branch of any milk-tree (*e.g.*, fig-tree, etc.) in the south-west corner under the *pandal*, and offers cocoanuts and plantains to the *pillaiyar*; then the bridegroom, in his full dress and ornaments, plants the branch, and seats himself on the *manavarei*. The *guru* utters some *mantras* and finishes the ceremonies.

'The bridegroom and the bride, in grand procession, go to the altar of their god, worship him, and break cocoanuts. Having come home, they sit on the *manavarei* facing the east, with the bride on the bridegroom's left. The *thali* is put in a little wooden box, the *guru* first blesses it, and sends it round the assembly to get the blessing of the old men present. This done, the *guru* receives the *thali* back, and, approaching the *manavarei*, orders the young couple to stand up, the bridegroom with his face towards the bride. The bridegroom now treads upon the bride's left foot with his right; a cloth is held between them as a veil; the bridegroom receives the *thali* from the *guru*, and puts it on the bride's neck from the other side of the veil, and his sister ties it round the bride's neck. Just at this time the drums are beaten and the trumpets blown, and the women who stand round raise a deafening shout.

'In the presence of the whole assembly the bride's father comes forward and says, "I have given my daughter in marriage to Mr. N——'s son." This he says three times, and pours water on the joined hands of the couple. After this they tie their hands with a coloured handkerchief.

'The bride and bridegroom are then seated upon two stools, and their respective friends pour milk on their heads, and give them sacred ashes with which to besmear their foreheads, and this they do. When all these ceremonies have been completed, the couple walk round the *manavarei* three times, and then retire into a room where the friends of the bridegroom sing adulatory songs.

'At night there is a procession of the young couple round the village in great pomp. On the third day a lighted candle is placed on the *manavarei*, a *pillaiyar* placed at the bottom of the lamp, and cocoanuts, plantains, betel and flowers offered to it, with a measureful of uncooked rice. The bride then bathes, and cooks some rice. The rice being ready, the bride and the bridegroom stand facing the east, and their friends take two dishes of the rice and wave them before the face of the couple, and then throw a handful of rice behind them to avert the evil eye; the remainder of the cooked rice is given to the barber and the washerman.

'A new plough is made by the carpenter, with which the bridegroom turns up the earth for about two or three yards around. The bride levels the earth thus turned up, and then sows some seed in it. The bride's brother pricks the bridegroom with an ox-goad, and the bridegroom's sister fills up the holes into which the bride had dropped the seed. While doing so the bride asks the bridegroom's sister: "Why do you fill the holes that I made?" To this she replies: "If you give your daughter in marriage to my son I will open them." Thus saying, she runs before the couple, and makes a feint of preventing them entering the house. When asked to open, she answers: "Yes, if you promise to give your daughter in marriage to my son." If her request is complied with, she opens the doors and lets them in.

'This is followed by a very unnecessary sort of farce. Under the *pandal* four sticks are placed so as to form a square, and a thread is passed round the four sticks; by the side of each of the sticks is placed a pot, one of which holds cunjee-water, another saffron-water, another sandal-water, and another betel. The bride's sister pours some from each of the pots on the bridegroom's head, who ejects betel-juice on her head in return.'

15. THE SHEPHERDS (*Eddaiars*).

Village shepherds are proverbially the most harmless and simple-minded folk of all the Indian tribes. The term *eddai* means 'middle,' as they were originally living in the land between the mountains and fertile plains, as it was a suitable place for grazing their cattle. There are 627,953 shepherds in South India. The occupation of this community is keeping cattle. They never intermarry with any other classes of Hindus. A few of them tend sheep and goats for the village landlords. But a large portion of them mind their own sheep and goats. They live in all parts of the land, and in every village they are welcome to fix their abode. Some of these men are employed as bearers of palanquins to the *Zamindars* (lords). As a rule, the men and women of this caste are very active and hard-working.

The shepherds' attachment to their sheep is very great, and they spend with them a greater part of the time, in the open fields, the thick forests, the rough hills, the grassy plains, and the deep valleys, in order to procure pasture for them. They sleep by turns in the open fields to watch their sheep. The heavy dew, the dust-storms, the dry western winds, the burning sun, the summer lightnings and thunder, the downpour of heavy rains, will not separate a shepherd from his sheep; they keep to them at all times and under all circumstances. The shepherds will often go and search for a lost sheep in the jungle and thick forest; sometimes they search the whole day, starving themselves, and even going without water to drink. We have ourselves seen, in our earlier days, shepherds carrying their lost sheep or lamb when they found it in the jüngle, and they have told us where they have been wandering for days together seeking their sheep that went astray. They never murmur, nor break the legs of the sheep, nor treat them unkindly.

India is subjected to frequent famines, during which time the shepherds suffer much in securing their own support and pasture for their cattle. We have seen the genuine self-sacrifices shown by the shepherds in the interest of their sheep during the memorable famine of the year 1877. They sold the few acres of land they possessed, and spent some portion of the proceeds on the support of their wives and children, leaving them in their native village, and starting off to distant districts for the purpose of finding pasture for their cattle. Travancore and other lands of hill tracts, was the place which attracted them, and there they remained till they heard that the rain had fallen in their own native country, and that there was grass and water again. They told us, after their arrival in their native country, of the hardship, the trial, the difficulty, they had to endure to protect the lives of their cattle and find pasture for them. The valleys of the vast ranges of the lofty mountains were the places of their sojourn. The nights they spent at the foot of these mountains they had bitter experiences. They were watching, one after another, to keep out the wolves and jackals and foxes, not to speak of the man-eating tiger, against whom they have to contend. For all these troubles nothing seems to take place to disturb the earnestness of purpose and calmness of mind with which they watch over their sheep.

The shepherds keep their folds in the night in the fields near the villages during the winter, but at other times they keep changing from field to field. One of the best methods of manuring the fields is to arrange for the sheep and goats to rest in them during the night; for this the landowners pay a certain amount in grain or money to the shepherds. This is the chief source of income to the shepherds. They eat, however, the flesh of the animals that die of natural causes, and drink the milk of the sheep. It is a remarkable thing among the shepherds that none of them will kill a sheep to eat its flesh, except on the occasions when they offer the rams as a sacrifice to their gods.

The shepherds, as a class, being very simple and ignorant, the devil-dancers and fortune-tellers make a good living out of them. Every now and then the shepherds will be brought within their clutches. If a child of a shepherd is sick the poor man goes to the fortune-teller or the devil-dancer to find out the cause of his child's sickness, and both of them agree in telling the shepherd that the sickness of the child is due to the anger of his family goddess, or else that some devil got hold of the child while it was playing under the tamarind-tree on a certain Friday afternoon. In both these cases the poor shepherd will have to spend some money either to drive the devil away or pacify the anger of his goddess. In the meantime the illness of the child will increase before they can fetch the wonderful native doctor, who comes with his medicines of herbs and plants, pills and powders.

There are several narratives given which serve to show the ignorance of these shepherds.

There was a shepherd, Valu by name, in a village situated at the foot of the western *ghats*. He followed the trade of his forefathers. One day he missed a certain lamb when counting his flock. At once he started off in search of this lamb. He wandered about till mid-day. At about 2 p.m. he came to a well, quite exhausted, in order to quench his thirst. When he began to look down into the well for the purpose of finding the steps, he saw a man in the well with the very lamb on his neck. The shepherd at once grew very angry with him. 'Oh, robber! I have got you at last; bring up my lamb, or else I will pelt you with stones,' said the shepherd, and stooped down to pick up stones with both his hands, when the lamb, which was on his own neck, fell down. Such was the wisdom of the shepherd.

There was a money-lender in a village who was in the habit of taking money to the different villages to lend the ryots, at enormous interest. On a certain day he took 100 rupees with him, and engaged a shepherd to go alone with him to a village situated near a hillock. The distance they had to travel was about twenty miles. They left about three o'clock in the evening. Before they had passed the tenth mile, they lost their way, and it was about nine o'clock at night. As they had to go through a jungle, the money-lender was afraid of the robbers, and told his companion, the shepherd, to lie down in some place without speaking a word or making any noise, while he went a little distance and hid himself under the bushes. About midnight a gang of robbers passed that way. One of them said: 'Look here! take care; here is a log of wood lying down on the way; don't knock against it.'

'Will a piece of wood in your village have five *panams* tied in a piece of cloth round its waist?' said the shepherd who was lying down. 'Oh, here is a fellow; catch him!' said the robbers. So they caught the shepherd, and snatched away the five *panams*, and left him, and went on their way. 'I wonder whether this money is false or true coin,' said one of the robbers. The shepherd, having heard this, called out to the robbers loudly: 'What do you mean? If you have any doubt about my coins, you had better find out whether they are true from the *chettiar* (money-lender), who is here by my side in the bush.' 'Ho! ho! there is another, is there? Catch him!' said the robbers. The *chettiar* was caught, and was beaten unmercifully, and the robbers went away with his 100 rupees, and the *chettiar* returned to his village in the morning, having learned a bitter lesson by taking an ignorant shepherd as his companion.

There was a king ruling over a fertile country. He had only a daughter, and to her he gave a liberal education. When the princess came of age the king asked her consent to be married to some one of the kings' sons of the neighbouring kingdoms; but the princess politely declined to marry any of the kings' sons unless they could equal her in mental attainments and other general accomplishments. This news got abroad among all the princes, and several of them applied and failed. At last one of the princes of a flourishing kingdom, and a master of Hindu literature, proceeded to the town where the famous princess was. The prime minister of the prince was a vain man, with a fondness for practical joking. He advised the prince not to marry the princess at all, but to humiliate her in some way. As they were nearing their destination, they got hold of a shepherd who was minding his sheep in a forest. They got the shepherd to shave his head and moustache, and they put on him the royal dress, placing him in one of the palanquins, and giving out to the people that he was the prince who was going to marry the celebrated princess. They gave strict orders to the shepherd to be silent. Whatever questions might be put to him by the princess or by any of her followers, he was only to point to the two schemers with his finger in answer to questions, as implying that the question must be directed to the prime ministers.

At length they entered the royal palace, and intimated to the king and princess their intentions. The shepherd, who was in a palanquin, was brought to the royal seat, and the disguised prince and prime minister played the part of prime ministers. The princess sent certain questions to the prince, who pointed to his followers to answer them. Finding his answers were correct, the princess was surprised at the attainments of the prime ministers, and thought how much more must be the attainments of the prince who had come to marry her. So the parties were agreed, and the wedding took place, after which the prime ministers left for their kingdom. The bridegroom entered into his chamber, and the bride, the princess, came to the chamber of the bridegroom with all her maids at a fixed lucky hour. When she entered the room she saw the prince fast asleep in his bed. She waited patiently at his bedside for several hours, but there was no sign of the prince getting up from his bed; in fact, he was still snoring. The princess attempted to awake the prince by sprinkling scent. The false prince was at the time dreaming that he was sleeping in the midst of his sheep, and when he felt the sprinkling of the scent, he cried, 'Hiss! away, you ram!' The princess was much surprised at this remark. Then she began to throw some flowers on him. Then he cried, 'Tush! get away, you foolish sheep!' Now the princess felt sure that something had gone wrong, and that there really must have been some mistake in her marriage. So she drew off her sword, and held it in her right hand, awaking the sleeping man with her left. As soon as the man was awake, she said: 'You tell me the truth about yourself, or I shall kill you.' The man was trembling while he confessed that he was but a shepherd, that he belonged to a distant village, and that the prince who had accompanied him took him by force, and made him enter into all these schemes. Immediately the princess gave money to the shepherd, and bade him run away from the palace, and then she put an end to her own life.

There is a custom prevailing among a certain class of shepherds which permits the daughters only to inherit the possessions of their fathers. The sons, when they are grown up, get married at the expense of the father, and then are sent to the wife's house with only the gift of a few sheep.

16. THE SWINEHERDS (*Kulavars*).

One of the wandering tribes of India is the *kulavar* or swineherd. This people are said to have followed Rama the Conqueror in his expedition against the King of Ceylon. They live in small portable huts, which they carry from place to place, but there are several camps of them scattered throughout the country. They are quite harmless, most ignorant, lazy, half naked, and ill fed; they are the gipsies of the plains. They keep herds of swine; their chief has a large number of followers, and a very large number of swine. To-day they will pitch their tent in one place, to-morrow they will remove it to another. They always pitch their tents near a tank in the centre of several villages, so as to give them a chance of getting into the villages in order to beg.

The women of the *kulavars* will go to the villagers' houses, and cry out, 'O Rama, Rama, Rama!' and repeat the word over and over again till the inmates of the house are moved to give them some alms, either in the shape of cooked meal or grain. The male members, while they are minding their swine, will be hunting wild rats. Towards the evening the women bring what they have begged to the huts, and the men turn up with some rats which they have caught. The women, when they go to beg, tie their babes on their back, hold a *soraikudukkai* (an Indian vegetable) in their left hand, and a small stick in their right.

Polygamy is rampant among this class. There are, however, some good men among them who desire to lead a better life. One of them has twenty wives, and he has regulated their daily life in the following manner: Ten of them must go to beg, five of them must mind the swine; the remaining five must be in his hut to attend to his personal comforts. One of these five must press his legs while he is lying down, another must keep his head clean, another must press his body, and the other two must be engaged in cooking his meals. The next day those who were minding the swine must remain in his hut, and those who were in the hut must go to beg, while five of those who went to beg must now go to mind the swine. So he changes the work of his wives every morning.

There are some *kulavars* who have married ten wives, and make them all beg for the food, while the husband enjoys his lazy life in the house.

The *kulavars* eat the pigs themselves, and sell a large number of swine to the people. Out of this money they buy their cloths, and spend for their marriage and other festivals. They worship devils and their departed relations, and make a special reference to those who are dead and buried. During festivals they dance through the whole night, and make a free use of liquor.

When a girl is young she is espoused to a young man. On the day of espousal a person is sent all round, wherever the huts may be, and when all are assembled the espousal is settled, and the bridegroom gives a feast of a fat pig and several bottles of arrack.

After this the espoused girl remains in her father's house until she has attained a suitable age or until the bridegroom is in a condition to provide for her.

On the day of marriage the bridegroom should give his father-in law three pigs of the value of three and a half rupees each ; or, if he cannot afford to give these, three fowls or a dog should be given as a *parisam*. Two pigs are killed for the feast. The young couple are seated upon a piece of wood inside a screen of cloth, holding each other by their little fingers. The parents of the couple mark their heads and foreheads with a mixture of pounded saffron and cotton-seeds, *chunnam* and rice. The bridegroom ties a little piece of silver of the value of eight or twelve annas round the bride's neck, and two new-coloured pots, filled with water, are placed before them, and a brass ring is put into each of them. The couple are ordered to take them out from the pots, and the one who first takes up a ring is reckoned the cleverer of the two.

The bridegroom takes hold of the bride's little finger, and leads her to his hut, and gives to his relation three *panams* as a present, and thus ends the ceremony.

17. THE BAZAAR-MAN.

There is no village in India which has not a bazaar of its own. If the village is large, there is a keen competition among the bazaar-men. The bazaar is a queer-looking place, having a room, with a narrow front, in which the bazaar-man sits, leaning against the wall. He has jaggery, chillies, coriander, saffron, pepper, cloves, dried ginger, tamarind, betel-nuts, tobacco, salt, onions, garlic, and a few other things which are required for the ordinary daily use of the villagers. Besides these, he keeps cocoanuts, plantains, dates, dried grapes, sugar, and sugar-candy for occasional use. During the harvest time he keeps a few extra things to attract the attention of the young folks, such as boiled pulse, nuts, sugar-cane, country buns, and cakes called *moorookoo*. The latter articles are greatly patronized by young folks of both sexes, who bring grain from the threshing-floor and cotton from the field to the bazaar-man, with or without the knowledge of their parents or guardians. Sometimes these village youths become indebted to the bazaar-men, who will let them have these articles on credit. When the payment is made the bazaar-man allows a free margin in measuring the grain or weighing the cotton which are brought by these young creditors.

The irregularity and confusion created by the bazaar-man when he sells his articles are very great. Mornings and evenings are the times in which the bazaars are over-crowded. The bazaar-man receives the money from the woman who comes to purchase salt and chillies, and he puts the money in his box and then makes the woman wait; he will ask the next person to give his money and inquire what he wants; then he will ask another person for his money or grain, and, having received this, he will ask another person to give his or her cotton, and he will yet again ask another to do the same. Having received all these, he will make them all wait, though each one is bawling out: 'Chettiar! chettiar! give me salt and chillies!' 'Give me jaggery!' 'Give me dried ginger!' 'Give me tamarind!' 'Give me pepper!' 'Give me pulse!' In the midst of this confusion and disorder the chettiar replies: 'Chee, poroo!' —*i.e.*, 'Wait, you dog!'—to every one of them. If the people bawl out still more, the bazaar-man grows furious, and asks one of the people: 'Rajatteeo? Poruka goodatho?'—*i.e.*, 'Have you become a queen? Can't you wait?' Then he asks yet another person to tell him what he wants. So, to see disorder and confusion, one needs to go to the village bazaar-man.

Another peculiarity of the village bazaar-man is that he seldom gives a definite reply to a person who wants a certain article if he has not got that article with him. Suppose Setu, a village doctor, goes to the bazaar-man, and asks him to give him an anna's worth of dried ginger; if the article is out of stock, 'I have got fine jaggery,' will be the reply of the bazaar-man. If the doctor again asks the bazaar-man to give ginger, and not jaggery, 'I have got new and good pepper,' will be the reply of the bazaar-man. After the third or the fourth time of asking, the doctor will come to his senses and understand that the bazaar-man has not got the article he wants in stock. For the bazaar-man to say that he has not got the article is regarded as a bad omen.

The village bazaar-man invests only some thirty to fifty rupees on his bazaar. With this capital he thrives and comfortably earns his bread.

There are some village bazaar-men who keep their stalls under trees, and in open fields, and sometimes they travel from place to place and keep their stalls in highways and public thoroughfares.

There is no particular caste or sect from which the village bazaar-men come. All castes and creeds of Indian people sell in the village bazaar, and they think themselves great merchants in their little world.

Some of the bazaar-men are very fond of hearing gossip from the women who come to make purchases. The stupidity of the thing is that while hearing the gossip the man makes the other customers wait.

III.

PROFESSIONS.

1. THE POET.

INDIA is famous for its poems, songs, and hymns. The innumerable medical works of the eighteen *sithathees* (devotees) are all written in verse. The descriptive accounts of the laws of the kings, with their commentaries, are poetical works. The great books on ethics, and the impracticable teachings of the Vedanta philosophy, are also to be classed as poetry.

If a beggar goes round begging, he will hold a harp in his hand and sing songs of praise to his gods and goddesses. The ordinary moral teachings and proverbs are all written in simple poetical style. The schoolboys in the villages, after learning their vernacular alphabet, are taught to read and write in poetry before they are taught to spell words of three syllables. It is not surprising, therefore, that we find so many village poets. Every village has a poet of its own, and they are generally poor men. The picture of an old village poet is given in illustration. He is holding his palm-leaves in his hand, and putting down his poetical thoughts with his peculiar pen. In the poet's house may be found several of these palm-leaf books. If a poet is in want of a daily meal he writes out a new poem in praise of some rich villager or bazaar-man.

On one occasion a village poet was lying down in his

house, and looking up at the sky through the thatched roof, a portion of which had been removed by the wind. He saw a heron flying over the top of the house, and addressed it thus: 'O heron! O heron! Hear the voice of the poet, whose house is uncovered, whose children are starving, whose wife is naked, and who is living in the kingdom of a flourishing and charitable king without being noticed by that king. Can you not at least tell the king of the country to which thou art going and bring me some help, bearing it on thy beautiful wings, and so save my life from death?'

The king of the country in which the poet lived happened to pass by the house that night in disguise. He heard the poem, and sent for the poet in the morning. He found him a really gifted poet, who had many excellent qualities, and therefore added him to the number of poets who were supported by the State.

These village poets travel from place to place at times, and sing songs in praise of well-to-do villagers, from whom they get temporary help. Some of these poets keep schools, and get a nominal fee from the boys, but it is hardly enough to keep their bodies and souls together. There is, however, a fine chance of getting a good gift from the villagers when they are asked to expound the great works of the Ramayana and the Mahabharata. This exposition is generally given during the summer months, when the harvest of the country is finished. That is the time for all kinds of amusements and pleasure-taking for the villagers. The poet who expounds the Ramayana or Mahabharata commences about eight o'clock at night, and keeps on till two or three in the morning. It is a remarkable thing that the village folk are found so attentive when these great works are explained. Of course, there are always some in the company who sleep while the explanation is going on; in fact, they are allowed to sleep if they like to do so. This kind of exposition lasts sometimes for six months, and even sometimes for twelve months, with a break in the middle. To pay for these expositions the villagers contribute each a certain sum, and present it to the poet when his work is finished.

Sometimes the poets are taken in procession in a *palkee*, with great Oriental pomp. On the last day of the exposition the well-to-do portion of the village present the poet with new cloths and gold rings.

In the large Indian villages where the ryots live the poets are well cared for. The children of the ryots are taught by the poet to expound carefully some of the poetical works, such as the *Naidatham*, or descriptive account of King Nalla and his wife Demayanti, the mother of beauty; the *Harischandra poorana*, or descriptive account of the King Harischandra, the truth-sayer, which is written in a very high style, and is exceedingly difficult to interpret.

We have often enjoyed the company of these poets when we have travelled through the villages. They never speak for more than five minutes without repeating some song, either of their own composing or composed by a friend. They have a song at their command for every conceivable thing and on every imaginable occasion, and the songs are often full of funny and witty anecdotes and sayings. Our own father was himself a village poet, and he wrote several songs, which we have still in our possession. There was, however, some difference in the case of our father, for he did not closely follow the customs of the village poets, seeing that he was a relative of a *Zamindar*, and a big landowner. We ourselves attempted to compose some songs in our early days. One song we composed in order to send to the father of the girl with whom we were in love before our marriage.

There is one great source of weakness in the village poets.

They know little or nothing of the grammar of their language; all they care for is to fill their brains with various poetical works, and store poems and clever sayings in their memories. In a sense we may compare them to the parrot, which can repeat only what it has been taught. Nevertheless, their power of imagination is remarkably developed. Their great fault is letting their imagination run riot on things which are both unreal and unsound. For instance, in describing the beauty of a woman, they compare her forehead to the new moon, her two arms to the loftiest heights of the Himalaya Mountains, her words to drops of honey, her voice to the Indian nightingale (*kuil*), and her general appearance to the appearance of a peacock. In praising a man, they will compare his house to the abode of the evening sun and moon, and the walls of the house to gold; the breaks of the roof to diamonds, the beams to silver, his garden to the birthplace of precious stones, his maidens to celestial beings, his enjoyments to the felicities of the gods themselves, his wife to the mother of wealth, his daughter to the mother of wisdom, and his sons to the rulers of the celestial world. If they begin to run down a man they will compare him to an ass, to a dog, to a monkey, to a buffalo, or to an unlucky woman, and his fields and houses are to be the abodes of thorns and thistles. And if they begin to curse a man they will say that the man will contract a loathsome disease, and his wife and his cattle will become barren. These cursing poems frighten the villagers greatly, and consequently they stand in awe of these poets, and do not like to offend them.

The Hindu Rajahs and Zamindars have their own poets, and some of them are celebrated men. For the support of these poets the princes will set apart several acres of land, and let them be cultivated free of rent. In some cases they

THE POET.

have given the profits of whole villages for their support. Many of them have received valuable gifts from princes, such as finger-rings and earrings, necklaces, silver or gold belts, palanquins, milking cows, horses, and lace cloths. In return, these poets compose new songs in praise of the prince or his family, in praise of the prince's particular hunting-dogs, horses, elephants, camels, quails, partridges, etc. When the prince goes to the jungle to hunt, his poet accompanies him, and he has to watch the movements of the prince, his followers, his dogs, and his horse. If a bison or deer or antelope has been shot by one of the followers of the prince, the praise has to be given to the prince in the song which celebrates the day's hunting, and not to the man who actually shot the animal. Flattery is not lacking in these poems. If the prince feels dull while he is in his palace, he sends for the palace poet, who comes into the presence of the prince, and amuses him and his courtiers with interesting or funny stories. One day, when we were present in a Hindu prince's palace, the poet related the following story: It appears that a jackal had been living for a long time under the foot of a lofty mountain, where all the big wild animals lived. The jackal often thought himself to be very weak, and the least influential animal in the mountain district. But one day he saw a magnificent elephant marching along the valley, and he coveted the flesh of that big animal. He ran to him, and prostrated himself before him, and begged him to listen to a message which he had to deliver. The elephant stopped, and asked the jackal what it was. 'Ah, I know,' said the jackal, 'that thou art the prince of thy race, and that there is no one equal to you in beauty and strength or fighting power. But how is it, I wonder, that a certain elephant of the other jungle always speaks disparagingly of you and of your noble family?' 'Does he?' replied the elephant; 'then I am not going to let that fellow alone; I will see him, and pay him off for his vain pride.' And so the elephant returned immediately to take his revenge. The other elephant was quietly standing at least a mile away. Before the elephant could find the road up to the place where that other elephant was, the jackal ran on before, saw the elephant, and spoke to him in the same strain. As soon as the two elephants approached each other they began to fight. They fought desperately for several hours, until at last one of them was killed. The jackal was hiding himself in the jungle, and watching the battle. He was delighted to see one of the elephants dead before him, and soon he began to eat the flesh of the softest part of the animal. The jackal was regular in his mode of preying on the animal, and so gradually worked its way into the creature's stomach. When these things happened, it was the summer season, the heat was very great, and the body of the elephant shrank while the cunning jackal was in the stomach eating to the full. After having had a really good feed, the jackal wanted to get out, but he found that the passage had so shrunk that it was impossible to force his way through.

Now the cunning jackal was caught, and could find no way of escape. At once he called out 'Sampo! Sampo!' The god Siva, with his wife Parvathy, happened to pass that way, and they saw the dead elephant in the jungle, and heard the voice coming from it. Siva went near the elephant, and asked the supernatural being who was within it to reveal himself to him. The being that was shut up in the stomach asked Siva to send for Indra, the god of rain. Siva, in order to please this being, at once sent for this god, and with him came heavy rain and wind. The body of the elephant, being well soaked with water, swelled, and gave an opportunity for the jackal to escape. In the meanwhile

Siva had invited all his celestial attendants to come and see this supernatural being who was in the belly of the elephant. When at last only a jackal came out, both the celestial beings and Siva had a hearty laugh before they went back to their world.

2. THE SCHOOLMASTER (*Wattiar*).

In every Indian village there is a school, or academy, which is known as the *pial* school. These academies are either conducted in the village inn or in a separate building, which is erected at the common expense of the villagers. It is usually a very plain and simple building with a thatched roof. The necessary annual repairs are attended to by the inhabitants themselves. There are no seats for the boys, nor books, nor slates. The books which are in use are written upon palm-leaves, and they are kept in a bookshelf belonging to each boy. These bookshelves are only two pieces of wood joined together with threads. At the top a hook is fixed. The boy, whenever he wants to take his books, lifts up the upper piece of the wood. He finds a place in the school to hang his bookshelf up. There may be fifty or a hundred of these shelves, or cases, hanging in the school when the school is opened. When the school is closed the boys take their bookcases to their respective homes.

It is the custom in the village schools for the boys to get up very early in the morning and to be at the school by four or five o'clock, without washing their faces or taking their morning meal. They must, however, have the marks of the sacred ash on their foreheads, as the token of their devotion

9

to the god Siva. The teacher himself comes at about six o'clock in the morning, drills the boys in their lessons for about two hours, and then dismisses them for their morning meal. The boys go away, and come back to school again at about nine o'clock. They keep on studying until twelve, when they are sent back for their noon-tide meal. They meet again at two, and the day's work closes at 6 p.m. During the school-time they are sent home one by one for drinking-water, or for other domestic reasons.

In the houses the boys are required to study until eight or nine o'clock at night, and they should bring a *chit* to the teacher from their relatives to show that they really were studying on the previous night. During this long course of study in the school the teacher appoints a grown-up boy, one of the most advanced scholars, to be a monitor, and he manages the school during the absence of the teacher. The boys, as a rule, spend about nine hours in the school, but the head-teacher spends at most four or five hours with them; during the remaining hours they are left entirely to the management of the monitor, who too often beats the children unmercifully, and treats them most cruelly. Those who have gained the favour of the monitor are allowed to play in the school, or to do nothing; or they are sent to fetch sweetmeats, which they gladly share with the monitor. But those who are not able to please the monitor are forced by him to study their lessons over and over again, and are not allowed to idle away their time.

The village teacher is not always a poet; he is usually a man of quite ordinary education, who has but little acquaintance with the grammar of his language, and is generally totally ignorant of geography, the history of the world, or the history of his own country. He does not know whether Windsor Castle is in the north of Africa or in the south of

Asia. He does not know that there are such things as the Red Sea, the Black Sea, and the Baltic Sea. He does not know whether Akbar, the Emperor, was the son of William the Conqueror or of Alexander the Great of Macedon. He cannot tell whether Jesus Christ was born in Judæa or in Abyssinia, or in Mexico, or in Lapland. But he knows that there are several milk oceans, fire oceans, ghee rivers, honey rivers, in the world, somewhere near the majestic Himalaya Mountains. He does not know whether the Empress of India has one or many sons; whether Her Majesty lives on curry and rice or bread-and-butter. Nevertheless, he knows that he is the schoolmaster of the village academy. Some of these village schoolmasters are good at arithmetic, figures and fractions being at their fingers' ends. Those who have gained a good education in the village schools under these teachers are generally clever in arithmetic.

The method of teaching in the village academy is very peculiar. The boys are asked to bring their lessons one by one. Some boys are allowed to write in the sand on the floor, some on the palm-leaves; some are studying their lessons; some are repeating their lessons to the teachers; some are undergoing punishment for not studying their lessons properly. The punishments of the boys are exceedingly severe. A boy under punishment is placed in a corner of the school, and required to stand on one leg while the other is bent and held in his hand. Here a boy is left a long time in a bending attitude; there another is made to sit and stand a hundred or even two hundred times in succession without ceasing. Another boy is hung up by his hands. While the boy is hanging a sharp knife is fixed on the ground, projecting upwards, so that he may not rest his feet on the ground. Sometimes the student is kept in a bending attitude, and another boy is made to ride on his back. And at times the student has to starve the whole day; and not infrequently the teacher unmercifully wields his cane of office.

In some schools the schoolmasters are old and helpless men, and they try to adopt the above plans in punishing their students. But these teachers are sometimes taught a useful lesson by the boys. The whole school is spread with sand, which is raised in a certain place. A palm-leaf mat is spread on this raised part, which forms the seat of the teacher. When the teacher grows furious, and comes down on the boys, some of the naughty ones combine together and scheme to hurt the teacher. When the teacher goes home to take his meal, these mischievous ones bring more sand, elevate the teacher's seat, and hide lots of thorns in it. As soon as their old teacher returns in the heat from his home, he usually rests awhile by lying down on the seat. He then orders some of the boys to press his legs, and some of them to fan him, so that he may have an hour's rest and good sleep. When the teacher goes to his seat and lies down on his back, he finds that something is pricking him through the mat, and so he turns this way and that way until his whole body is pricked by thorns. Of course the teacher gets up, and punishes the wicked lads, and takes special care about his seat in the future. Still, the boys will continue to trouble him in some way.

All the village teachers are in the habit of taking snuff. Our old friend, when he is hard up, sends one of the students to fetch some snuff from the bazaar. The student keeps a snuff-box full of cayenne-pepper or chillie-powder, which he brings, and leaves gently on the seat of the teacher. The teacher, in a hurry, takes a large pinch of snuff and inhales it, and then has a dreadful burning sensation in his nose and brain. Tears flow down; he coughs over and over again. 'Oh, great sinner! big fool!' he cries, but at his distress the students roar with laughter.

The school-fee is collected from every boy in the school, some paying from twopence to sixpence, others a few measures of grain, and others pay in kind. When a boy is newly admitted his parents send some money, according to their circumstances. Before the alphabet is taught to the new-comer the teacher expects to receive an offering from the parents, either plantains, cocoanuts, fried rice, or betel-nut. These are placed before the god in whose presence the initiation ceremony takes place. If the income of a school is insufficient for the maintenance of the schoolmaster, the village gives the teacher some measures of grain during the time of harvest. The schoolmaster will sometimes send the boys in charge of the monitor to sing through the streets of the village, and beg some oil, chillies, and cow-dung from every house, and these the teacher takes home for his own use. The teacher and the pupils go about once a year for a week or two to collect money from the villagers to make *pooja* to Sarasvathy, the Goddess of Knowledge. This is a good time both for the pupils and for the teachers. The parents of the students take special care to purchase new cloths for their children, and dress them as neatly as possible in quite an Oriental fashion. On this occasion they are instructed by the teacher to sing action-songs. Out of the collection that is made the teacher takes the lion's share, and the remainder is spent in giving a treat to the children on the *desara,* or festival days.

Learning in the village academy is a very tedious and heavy business, so the pupils anticipate with pleasure the holiday times. These they get at both the new moon and the full moon for two days. Besides these four monthly holidays, the important Hindu festival days are also observed as holidays. The day on which a new-comer is admitted to a school also becomes a holiday after the ceremony is over. There are no long holidays in the village academy except at the beginning of the year, when they have four or five days.

The curriculum of the village academy includes the alphabet, which is often one year's study; the multiplication-table; arithmetic, including fractions; proverbs; sayings; dictionary; composition; writing—all this is for ordinary students. For the advanced there is 'Kural,' a great work on ethics, 'Bharatta,' 'Ramayana,' and 'Naidatham.' In a few village schools grammar is also taught. If a boy enters the village academy at the age of seven, he is kept there till the age of sixteen or eighteen. If he is studious and smart he can master all the subjects above mentioned.

Now, under the British Government, local fund schools are opened in a few villages of certain districts, and a better system of education prevails. The missionary bodies of different denominations also have village schools, which are conducted in a better style. But all this is a mere drop in an ocean. It will be a hopeful time when every village has a good school, in which elementary history, geography, science, and religion may be taught.

3. THE PHYSICIAN.

There are two or three physicians or doctors in each village, but they do not belong to any particular sect or caste. Sometimes the barber also practises medicine.

Sometimes a Vellala or a Brahmin will become the doctor of the village. The study of medicine is a prolonged business. There is no school or college which gives special medical instruction, but there are countless works on medicine, which have been written by the eighteen doctors of medicine of ancient times. Some of their names are Agastiar, Thaarayar, Bogar, Konganavar, Machamuni, Tholkappiar. It is a life-long study to master all these medical works, and to learn how to practise their rules, as they are written in a technical language. Those who have studied these works carefully find themselves with some effective medicines at their command, and they are often very successful in healing the sick. They administer different kinds of *laghiumo* and *thailams* for different diseases, especially to improve and purify the blood. If any of them find out a specific, they use it during their lifetime, but will not reveal it to any other doctor. When the finder dies, the remedy also dies with him. The doctors are able to make some fine powders and pills from nine kinds of poisons. They use copper, iron, gold, quicksilver, mica, pearls, and corals. These are usually administered only to the rich and the noble; but some of these medicines also help the physicians in treating the diseases of the common folks. There are some fine decoctions made of various herbs, seeds, roots, leaves, and barks. These are often very effective, and bring almost instant relief to the sufferer. Ginger and dried ginger are frequently used for various kinds of disease, but especially for diarrhœa, indigestion, rheumatic complaints, cold, and fever. Pepper is used for cough, and for clearing the throat. Chillies or cayenne-pepper is a wonderful remedy for rheumatic pains and swellings. Besides these, the doctors make ointments from onions, eggs, snakes, frogs, wild rats, and they make use of them as remedies for serious sickness. These physicians cure fever, dysentery, rheumatic pains, headache, earache, toothache, eye-diseases, skin-diseases of all kinds, bronchitis, cold, in some ease snake poison, dyspepsia, and other ordinary diseases, and they have remarkably efficient remedies for all kinds of venereal diseases. But they make fatal mistakes when the patients get organic diseases, such as heart, liver, and lung complaints. The steam-bath in a primitive form is used by these physicians in certain cases; but leprosy, consumption, and lunacy are quite incurable by them.

The patients who are under the treatment of these village physicians have to undergo very trying diet, especially if the patient is suffering from fever. In some cases the physicians require the patients to abstain from certain things for a period of forty days.

To find out the symptoms of a disease, they feel the pulse in the morning, noon, and evening. Then they decide the nature of the sickness. The village doctors consequently get into a delightful muddle. If a man is suffering from heart-disease, they are sure to treat him for headache. If a woman is suffering from some disorder of the womb, they are sure to treat her for stomach-ache. If a man is suffering from consumption, they will order him an oil-bath twice a week, as they believe that his body is over-heated. Their knowledge of anatomy is most imperfect and limited, and this accounts for their constantly misjudging the nature of the disease.

The worst class of village physicians are the men of only ordinary knowledge in the art of medicine, and this, unfortunately, is the class that is represented in most of the Indian villages. They have no real knowledge of medicines, and those which they use are very few and simple; but their charges for the medicine and their fees for attendance are also very low. They have pills for all kinds of diseases that can be thought of. These medicines they keep in a cloth bag, which is carried under their arms wherever they go. Ten out of a hundred patients who are suffering from serious diseases will be sure to lose their lives, and so one of their pills is sarcastically called 'Vaigunda-mattira,' *i.e.*, 'The pill that sends into the other world.' As most of the villagers are very poor, the cheapness of the remedy is important, and they readily call in the quacks, who will receive fourpence or perhaps sixpence for the medicine, or perhaps a shilling for all their visits; or it may be they will take a hen, both for their medicine and their fee. But these cunning 'angels of death' often demand a separate and extra sum for pretending to drive the devil from a sick patient. When the patient is dead, these physicians put the blame upon the departed man's relations, accusing them of not watching the patient, or not observing closely the diet which was prescribed. There are many persons, both young and old, who complain of having lost their upper teeth, or the lower teeth, or grinders, or even the whole set, by taking medicine from these doctors. They are accustomed to administer quicksilver which has not been properly purified. Thousands of the people in India die for want of proper medical aid. The Government has opened local fund dispensaries in some centres, and these are a great boon; but there are still thousands of villages which are left to the tender mercies of these incompetent quacks.

The village optician is remarkably clever in attending to eye diseases. When a person is suffering from cataract or other eye-disease, he invites the optician to attend on him, and he receives a fee from the patient according to his circumstances. He operates on the eye with his crude knife, and applies his rough iron bars, eight inches long, to the eye. Doubtless the patient is often left to tell the sad story of his eyes being lost through the bungling of the optician. These opticians travel from village to village, with the result of making many people blind. Out of the 50,000 blind persons in South India there are few who have become blind through natural causes. Now the news is getting abroad that eye-diseases can be cured in the Eye Infirmaries of the cities, and sometimes the richer classes in the villages avail themselves of this opportunity.

There are dentists who often have an extensive practice through a district. If a person complains that he or she has toothache, these dentists apply some paste to the jaw, and give some powder with which to cleanse the teeth. If this does not cure they make the patient inhale steam, and this will often bring instant relief. In some cases the dentist is asked to pull out the tooth which causes the pain. He then takes out his pincers and nips a tooth, most probably not the decayed one, but the next to it. His mode of drawing it out causes great agony, and sometimes is even followed by death.

There are also village surgeons. The surgery of the village is chiefly practised by the barbers. For severe wounds they apply cold water. They wrap up the part well with cloth and pour cold water on it for hours together. In this way they often succeed in healing the wound.

In the villages where the Mohammedans live the surgeons are the men who effect the act of circumcision. They bring round their patient after the operation by applying cold water to the wound.

India being a country of extreme heat, piles are a common disease among those who constantly expose themselves to the sun, as the tillers of the soil must do. Those who live on alluvial soil and drink saltish water suffer from the painful sickness occasioned by internal or external piles. There are hundreds, both of men and women, who suffer from this irritating disease. The pile doctors are clever men in their way, and they get a good living, as they have their headquarters in one village, and travel about the country. They demand a fixed fee from every patient, no matter whether he is rich or poor. They apply some poisonous stuff, bandage the part well, and allow it to remain for three days. On the third day the piles are found to have decayed, and they may even have fallen away, leaving a large hole, and this has to be healed by the specialist, who applies some medicine and gives good nourishment. In this way the pile specialist is successful in many cases, but the poison may get into the system if it is applied in excess, and then blood-poisoning follows and the patient dies. It is always a case of life or death with the village pile-doctor.

There are several works written on cattle disease, and there are specialists who have studied these works and treat the various diseases of the cattle. Some of them are very successful veterinary surgeons. The worst part of the treatment of animals is branding them with red-hot iron bars on all parts of their bodies; and even worse still is their trying to decorate the animal with ornamental marks made with the heated iron. The village veterinary surgeon appoints a time for seeing sick animals once or twice a week, and there is always quite a multitude of them waiting for treatment. There will be cows and bullocks and buffaloes, and often also sheep and goats. For all the sicknesses of these useful domestic animals the village veterinary surgeon has only one grand remedy—branding of the legs, faces, and bodies of he beasts.

Sometimes the veterinary surgeon will be busy from six in the morning to six in the evening, with only one short break in the interval for a meal. He receives a fixed fee for every animal he attends. He makes use of the men who bring the cattle to heat the irons. Having accomplished his first and last operation, he advises the owner of the bullock, cow, or buffalo to mix certain herbs with the cotton-seed which he gives to the animal. Doubtless this is the remedy that really cures the animal. We wish the Society for the Prevention of Cruelty to Animals would interfere in the matter, and put a stop to this cruel and useless custom of branding.

4. THE PRIEST.

There is no village in India without its priest. The people themselves believe that they ought not to live in a village where there is no *koil*, *i.e.*, the house of a god. Every village *koil* has a priest of its own, who attends to the many duties of the *koil*, no matter whether it be a Sivan *koil* or a Vishnu *koil* or a Pillayar *koil*, or a *koil* belonging to some local god or goddess. The duties of the village priests are not simple and easy, but they do not require any great skill or profound learning. There are two classes of village priests—the one Brahmin, the other non-Brahmin. The former are acknowledged as the proper priests of the village. They may serve in a village temple or not, but they have the right and privilege of enjoying an annual income from the people. It is not necessary that these priests should live in the village where they attend to their duties. They may live in a more suitable and convenient one, and this they often do, visiting other villages whenever there is work for them to do. Each priest is usually in charge of more than one village.

The villagers go to their priest in order to consult him about business matters which they have in hand. If there are marriages to be arranged, they ask the priest to examine the horoscope of both the young man and the young woman who want to be married. They consult him to fix a day for beginning to plough, to fix a day for sowing, and to fix a day in which to begin the harvest. Before they start on a distant journey they ask the priest to fix a day on which they can get the smile of a good star. They consult him when a child is born, a girl attains her womanly age, or when a person has fallen sick. They invite the priest to perform their marriage ceremony, their funeral ceremony, and the anniversary of a relative's death. The service of the priest is also needed in all the purification days, and in the opening of a new building. On all these occasions the priest receives offerings in the shape of money, rice, paddy, vegetables, milk, *ghee*, fruits, plantain-leaves, etc. These things form the staple food of a Brahmin priest; hence he is not imprudent in collecting such necessaries of life. As he is a vegetarian, he never demands a hen or a lamb. He is always on the look-out, and moving frequently among the villagers, in order to remind them of the approaching *thithi*, or annual ceremony for the dead. Through these ceremonies the Brahmin priests make large incomes.

These ceremonies were introduced many centuries ago, and their object is to secure the forgiveness of the sins of the departed father, mother, or forefathers of the man who spends his money in getting the ceremony performed. Before this annual ceremony day comes round, the priest gives to Ramasamy a long list of things to be bought. On the day of the ceremony the priest and his male relations reach Ramasamy's house at about 9 a.m. By the time the priest arrives, Ramasamy and his household, having bathed and dressed themselves in clean cloths, are ready to receive him. They first take him into a spacious room or hall, in which there are twenty-one plantain leaves spread out on the floor, each of these being filled with six measures of rice, heaps of vegetables of all kinds, plantains, pulse, *ghee*, curds, honey, new cloth, money, and other things. The twenty-one leaves represent the twenty-one departed forefathers of Ramasamy, and the priest freely, willingly and gladly pronounces forgiveness of all the sins of omission and commission which have been charged to those twenty-one departed souls of the forefathers of Ramasamy. If Ramasamy is a man of limited means, he only supplies three leaves to the priest, and then the priest can see his way clear to forgive the sins of only *three* of the departed souls of Ramasamy's ancestors, his parents and his grandfather. If Ramasamy is a rich man, he can get the sins of any number of his departed ancestors forgiven, provided he can supply plantain-leaves full of good things, in the name of his forefathers. The priest readily forgives the sin of any man who can give him a good offering.

It is regarded as a great sin for a villager to receive anything from a Brahmin priest free of charge; but it is a blessing to him to give anything that he has. If a man has a fine black cow, it is considered advantageous for him to give it to the priest, and in return to receive the forgiveness of all his own sins as well as those of his forefathers. It is inculcated by the priest that it is a sin to keep a *black* cow in the village. The Brahmin priest consequently gets an income on which he can live very comfortably. Of course, his Aryan blood and his long ages of civilization and culture, give him an important position in village society. He is really the most intelligent man in the village, and he has introduced several useful institutions in the name of religion, for which the villagers ought to be thankful. Wherever the institutions and regulations of the priest are observed, the savageness and vulgarity are certainly moderated.

The union, craftiness, precaution and intelligence of the earlier village priests were so great that they induced the ancient village rulers to establish charitable institutions for their own sole benefit and for that of their posterity. These institutions are continued from one generation to another, and they are now enormously wealthy. There are several *chatrams*, *i.e.*, inns; there are innumerable temples, which have great endowments, consisting of lands, villages and money; the income arising from the property is entirely consumed by the priests. Having these privileges, the priests have too often dishonoured the true religious life, and become carnal-minded. In many cases they have altogether lost the true conception of God and of the life that is pleasing to Him. They have, as it were, paralyzed their religious ceremonies and devotions, and grown ever more licentious through materializing their religion. They multiply their institutions, and often seriously differ from one another in their teachings, and they cause the people to go to all sorts of unnecessary expenditure, and so they suck the life-blood out of the people. Having secured a large income, the priests sit down to enjoy their curry and rice, pulse and *ghee*, in quietness with their families. It is unfortunately also the case that they utilize their incomes in supporting concubines. The worst of the Hindu system is the support of public prostitution in connection with the

Hindu temples. Women have the privilege of dancing and singing before the processions of Hindu gods, and supporting themselves from the temple funds. These village priests are not, perhaps, much worse than the Druid priests of ancient Britain, or the learned priests of ancient Egypt, Greece or Rome.

One of the important institutions of the priests is *Brahmana bojana*, *i.e.*, the feeding of Brahmins. This takes place either in a large *chatram*, or in a temporary shed which has been erected for the purpose at the expense of a rich villager. This rich villager sends out invitations to the Brahmins of the different villages to attend the feast. Having done this, he engages the priest of his own village to manage the feeding of the Brahmin guests. If the Brahmins know in time—as they generally do—that there is going to be a 'feeding of Brahmins' in such and such a village, they actually eat little or nothing for two or three days, and thus keep themselves in readiness for a good feed.

At the appointed hour all assemble—none but Brahmins. Perhaps it will be a gathering of a hundred, or even two hundred, people of both sexes. The villager who has undertaken to feed them supplies several earthen vessels full of *ghee*, curds, buttermilk and milk, some measures of honey, a large quantity of sugar, and all sorts of fruit and other necessaries, such as rice, curry-stuff, vegetables, plantain-leaves, sago, *pappadams* and asafœtida. The cooking is all done by the Brahmins themselves, asafœtida and *mulukutanny* being used as substitutes for the brandy and wine of the West. This host of Brahmin guests feed themselves well, so much so, indeed, that they are often unable to get up from the floor and walk as far as the back-yard to wash their hands. All the good things that were prepared for them have found ready consumers, and the guests can seldom walk, in the evening, to their respective villages, because of their heavily-laden stomachs. The saying that the 'Brahmin is a *bojana pirya*,' *i.e.*, 'the Brahmin is fond of eating,' is verified on such occasions.

There were, on one occasion, two Brahmin feeding-parties in a village, and each party, having done justice to their calling, returned to their respective homes. One of the Brahmins of the party who had their feeding-place on the west was making his way towards the east, and another Brahmin, who had his feeding with the eastern party, was going up to the western side. They met midway. One of them had a pair of shoes on his feet, but he was not able to look down to see whether he was really wearing them or had left them in the feeding-house; and so, as soon as he saw the other Brahmin coming towards him, he addressed him thus: 'O friend, do you see a shoe on my foot?' Unfortunately, that Brahmin also had enjoyed a good feeding, like his brother, and he, too, was unable to look down at the foot of the Brahmin. He looked round about, here and there, towards the sky. 'Ha! I do not see the pair of shoes there.' Such was the helpless condition of these two Brahmins who were returning from the scene of 'feeding the Brahmins.' It is said that a Brahmin, not knowing how much to eat in a feeding company, ties round his stomach a piece of thread, and eats until the thread bursts with the distension of the stomach.

There are also non-Brahmin priests in the villages who are in charge of the temples of the local gods and goddesses. These priests bathe in cold water very early in the morning, and then go to the flower-gardens and pluck flowers and leaves; these they boil with a measure or half a measure of raw rice in a brass vessel, and place the same, together with a broken cocoanut, flowers, etc., before the image. They

10

then wave incense and ring the temple bell. On hearing this the people of the village, wherever they may be, raise both hands towards the temple. Sometimes the villagers go to the temple, when the priest performs the *pooja*, which takes place twice a day. It must be remembered that these priests serve in the temples which are consecrated to the minor gods, who are very numerous in the villages.

The expenses of the daily *pooja* are met by the gifts and offerings of the villagers, and also by the revenue accruing from the endowment of the temple. The annual festival will cost from 100 to 150 rupees, and this sum is collected among the villagers themselves by compulsory subscriptions. If there is any surplus left after spending for the annual festival, that is added to the general fund of the temple.

The priest is constantly going about among the people, and telling them of the wonderful things that have been done by their gods to this or that person. By interpreting dreams as visions given to the people by the gods, he is constantly inducing somebody to pay a special vow to the gods. He gets the money, and makes the necessary preparations for the special *pooja*. This extraordinary *pooja* is performed by the priest simply by adding some extra ceremonies to the ordinary course. On these occasions people assemble to receive the answers to their prayers, which are supposed to come through the medium of lizards. Some of them wish to know the will of their god in regard to some particular matter which they have in their minds. For instance, if Gopal desires to marry Soundry, he comes to the temple to get information from the god as to whether that marriage will prove a success or a failure. He tells the priest that he desires to know the will of the god concerning a certain matter, without letting him know what it is. The priest at once goes to his private chamber, takes one red flower and one white one, puts each in a separate leaf, rolls them round and ties them well; then the priest brings these two small bundles and leaves them at the foot of the image. Then he tells Gopal to take one of these bundles, and says to him: 'If the god is willing to answer you favourably, he will give you the white flower; and if he is not willing to give you a favourable answer, you will get the red flower.' At once Gopal prostrates himself before the image, and takes up one of the bundles, which he gives back to the priest. He opens it in the presence of Gopal and the others who may be present in the temple. If the flower happens to be the white one, then Gopal leaps for joy; but if it is the red one, he goes away low and dejected. There may be many others present who are also anxious to know the will of the god about some matter of personal or family interest. The priest adopts the same plan in revealing the will of the god to them, but sometimes he will point out to them the right side of the temple on which to get a favourable answer through the lizard. People will wait for hours together for the answer of the lizard. There may come the voice of the god through the lizard on either the one side or the other, but it is oftener on the right side, for the priests are careful to kill the lizards on the left side of the temple building when the people assemble to know the will of their god.

These non-Brahmin priests cannot get as much income from the people as the Brahmin priests can. Nevertheless, they lead a very easy and comfortable life at the expense of the villagers. This class of priest is not cultured or intelligent, as the Brahmin priests are, and consequently they sometimes have to cultivate their lands in order to meet the demands of their families. They believe in matrimonial transactions, and some of them are men with large families, and their male descendants become their successors.

5. THE MUSICIAN.

No joyful or sorrowful occasion in a village passes without an accompaniment of music. They have music on the day of their marriage, and music in connection with their deaths. They must have music at the purificatory ceremony of a girl who has attained her womanhood. They cannot make their united offerings to their gods and goddesses without music. No ceremony, no festival of the village, can go on without a musical accompaniment.

There are three kinds of music, the *paray kottoo*, *pallan kottoo*, and *raja malaam*. The *paray kottoo* is a very peculiar kind of music. It is played by the pariahs, the out-caste people of Southern India. There are four or five round drums, and one or two Indian trumpets. These instruments make up the full set of the *paray malaam*. When the men beat the deafening drums and blow the trumpets, it is enough to rend the air, to frighten the children, and to drive the beasts from the neighbouring forests. These musicians know no tunes, and all that they do is jump hither and thither while they beat the drums. The villagers are not expected to pay anything when these pariahs are asked to play, but they have to feed them.

The *pallan kottoo* is very little better, either in sound or in method. There are two or three drums and a country clarionet, and with these the *pallars* keep on playing only one tune of their own through the whole day, and even sometimes through the night. If these musicians commence to play in the night, the sound will be heard two or three miles away, and it has a charming effect upon the uncivilized masses. These musicians also render their services for little or no payment when they are required by the villagers.

The *raja malaam* is a far superior kind, and the most decent of all the three musical sets. It is owned by a class of people called *Octhan*, who are allowed to move about freely in the inner and outer yards of the village houses. This musical set consists of two or three drums of a peculiar shape, which are beaten only on one side, and a drum which can be beaten on both sides, a cymbal, two clarionets, and an instrument called *othos—i.e.*, helping instrument—which keeps only one note, like the drone of a bagpipe. These instruments form the whole set of *raja malaam*. These men know several tunes, and they also understand the notes of the Oriental music, but they cannot be classified as experts in the art of music. They also play some Mohammedan tunes. This set of musicians cannot be found in every village, and they have to be engaged by the party who requires their service for a fixed sum of money, which must be paid promptly at the close of their service. During marriage times there is usually a great demand for this kind of music.

6. THE MONEY-LENDER (*Muthalallie*).

The evils attendant on borrowing money are not unknown to the villagers of India. There are scores of people who are in the clutches of the money-lenders, who try desperately to get out of their hands, but fail in their attempts. There are both general and special causes which account for the villagers running into debt. The entire energy and enterprise of the villager is put into agricultural pursuits. There is not a soul in the villages who can boast of being a manufacturer of any useful article. Consequently, money is not passing into the hands of these people at all seasons of the year, but only at the harvest-time. They are consequently driven in the time of necessity to the money-lender. The ignorant and heavily-burdened villagers have many occasions for getting small or even large loans at exorbitant interest. They must borrow money to meet the demands of the tax-gatherers; they must seek for loans, mortgaging their lands or their jewels, in order to perform the marriages of their sons and daughters. In some cases they cannot manage to perform the funeral ceremonies without getting into debt. And, over and above all, they cannot be quiet, but must commence a lawsuit of some kind against either friend or foe, in order to teach him a lesson for his bad behaviour at a marriage, or on the occasion of a village festival. In such ways the villagers become the slaves of those creators of misery, the money-lenders.

The more prominent class of the people that is engaged in the business of money-lending is called *Năttookŏttay chetties*. They live in the village of Năttookŏttay and its surroundings, in the Madura district; from thence they travel all over the country, and they have even gone to the Indian

MONEY-LENDER.

colonies, in order to ply their money-lending tricks on the poor villagers who have left their homeland to try and make their fortunes. The habits and modes of living of this class of money-lenders are simple and plain. They have fine, substantial, stone-built houses in their villages, in which the female members of their families remain when they go on circuit. These females have very few jewels, and they are savage-looking, illiterate, and little more than half clothed. The men have clean-shaved, bald heads, big holes in their ears, a shrewd, business-like appearance, and a black skin. They belong to the Siva sect, but their sympathies go towards any Hindu temple and any charitable objects of the Hindu community. They are very united among themselves. If a man belonging to their community fails in business, all the others contribute a small sum per head, and the amount will reach about 40,000 or 50,000 rupees at the lowest. One of them will then take the fallen man, and the money that has been given to him by their community, and make him a partner in his business. They have also a general charity fund, to which every member of the community must contribute three per cent. of his annual profits. This fund is swelling to an enormous amount, and it is kept under the management of an influential person of their community, who lends it out at interest.

Their dealings with village communities are ruinous. They have the 'deceitfulness of riches'; they 'devour widows' houses'; and they freely spend a certain portion of their income in embellishing the pagodas of the famous Hindu shrines. There is no class that can equal them in craftiness. They know the ins and outs, the needs and wants, of the people, and are always on the watch for the most favourable occasion on which to further their own interests. If two brothers are fighting for their rights after the death of their father, the money-lenders step between them and render such financial help as enables them to bring their dispute into the law-courts. Of course, they charge twenty per cent. compound interest on the money they have lent. Probably the fighting of the brothers will continue for about seven years, the case passing from the lower courts to the highest tribunal in the land. During that period thousands of rupees have to be spent. At last, when their disputes are settled, there are heavy debts to clear. In winding up the accounts they discover that their property is only just enough to pay their debts, and that pauperism is the only thing left for them.

The many village chiefs, landlords, *zamindars*, who have become the miserable victims of these avaricious money-lenders, are living monuments of the misery caused by them. They remind one of the monkey who settled the dispute between the two foolish cats.

There were two cats in a village, which got hold of a lump of sugar-candy and took it to the meadows. As soon as they reached the grassy slopes they began to fight for the sugar-candy. Each of them wanted to consume the whole of it. While the fight was going on, there came a monkey and spoke thus to the cats: 'Peace be to you. What is the matter that you are fighting about? Tell me, please.' 'This sugar-candy is mine,' said one of the cats; but the other declared that it was his. 'Well, then, you both, my friends, seem to have a share in the candy. Let me help you by dividing it. Bring me a pair of scales, please,' said the disinterested monkey. The scales were brought at once by one of them. Holding the scale in his hand, the friendly monkey divided the sugar-candy, and placed the two pieces, one on each pan of the scale. The cats were most thankful to find such a wise and ready helper. The monkey, in weighing, found that one portion of the sugar-candy was a little heavier than the other, so he tried to make them equal by cutting off a piece of it and throwing it into his mouth. And now he saw that the other portion was a little heavier than the one which he had tried to adjust, so he cut off a piece of that and threw it into his mouth. Again he found an inequality between the two shares, and therefore he repeated the process of adjusting the scale until he had consumed the whole of the sugar candy, little by little. 'After all, I took only my share for the trouble which I have taken in dividing the sugar candy for you, my dear cats. Now I can do nothing for you but wish you every success. Good-morning,' said the monkey, and went on his way.

This illustration is precisely applicable to the village money-lenders, who step in between parties who are fighting over their properties. They are sure eventually to get them out of their hands.

These money-lenders have another evil habit: they spoil young men who are of age, and are living a profligate life while under the management of their parents. For instance, if the money-lender hear of a wealthy man's son, he induces him to borrow money without the knowledge of his parents. A document is prepared and executed by the young man for a loan of, say, 30,000 rupees, and the document is duly registered at the registrar's office, the money-lender paying the full amount of the loan to the young man in the presence of the registrar. When the parties have got out of the office, the money-lender takes back the sum of 20,000 rupees from the young man, and sends him off with only 10,000 rupees. At the due time the money-lender files a suit to recover a sum of 45,000 rupees, to which the loan has swelled with the added interest. This demand of the court alarms the rich father, who redeems his son in quite an honourable way, and thus saves his own reputation. But the loss he sustains by the wicked dealings of the money-lender with his son is ever after a most painful memory to him.

This money-lending class are always busy in devising schemes and plans that will further their own interest and ruin the interests of others. Their faults are many, and their virtues are few. The most prominent of the latter is their completing temple buildings left unfinished by Hindu kings and chiefs, and supporting the Hindu temples. All the temples in India have ready, generous, and munificent helpers in the money-lending *Nāttookōttay chetties.* Within the last twenty-five years several famous but ruined temples and pagodas have been rebuilt, repaired, modified, and improved by them at the cost of lakhs of rupees. They have also built several *chatrams* (inns), and have left great endowments for the support of the Brahmin priests, in several parts of the country. Probably there is no class of people in the whole of India who take such an interest in spending their money for objects connected with the Hindu temples.

There are also small local money-lenders, who lend out money or grain on a small scale, and receive the same back at the time of harvest, with high interest. The proposed village agricultural bank will prove specially helpful to the imperilled agricultural classes in the village communities.

7. THE DEVIL-DANCER (*Payade*).

The devil-dancers should be regarded as a third class of village priests. But, as their vulgarity and peculiarity need particular consideration, it is better to treat them under this distinct heading.

There is no sect or class of people who take to this calling; but the most ignorant, vulgar, well-built and lazy scoundrels act this part. The temples which are consecrated to devils are often arranged without a roof, being only an enclosure of bare walls. In some cases they have a small covered building attached. There is no special endowment for the support of these devil temples, nor any regular establishment. One or two villagers will unite in undertaking the work of devil-dancing. On a fixed day of the year, a certain section of the villagers, if not all, assemble together, and bring their offerings and their vows to the devil-temple. They erect a temporary shed to accommodate them for one night, and decorate this temporary building with plantain-trees, evergreen-leaves, flowers, and tender cocoanuts. They also engage a party to play that peculiar drum which helps the devil-dancer to go mad. Men and women who come to the festival commence by boiling rice in a number of vessels—each vessel representing a family. The images which are in the devil temple have each before them heaps of plantains, broken cocoanuts, sugar-canes, flowers, limes, and arrack bottles. Lambs or cocks are sacrificed, and placed at the sides of the images. At about ten o'clock the devil-dancers appear before the people with peculiar long caps on their heads, brass bangles on their hands and legs; they wear a peculiar *pandalam*, full of bells, and devil-images and garlands of flowers are round their necks. These monsters help themselves freely to the bottles of arrack placed before the images, and then they dance like devils. They bawl out 'Ho! ho!' with all their strength; the beaters of the drum get tipsy, and then all join together and dance till one o'clock in the morning, at which time the devil-dancers pretend to show the manifestation of the devils to the people. The cleverest and strongest and youngest among them steps forward with a chutty full of rice and blood of lambs. He mixes these well together, and makes the substance into large and small balls. Holding the vessel in his left hand, he bawls out again 'Hai! hai! hai!' and starts off immediately for the cremation-ground. A man holding a torchlight in his hand and another man beating a drum follow the devil-dancer. He runs hither and thither on the cremation-ground, pretending that he throws off the balls of rice into the sky so that they may be devoured by the devils. In reality he simply dodges the two fellows by saying, 'There is the devil!' or 'Here is the devil!' 'Lo, an army of devils in the sky!' These statements, and the tremendous noise made by the devil-dancers, stupefy the two fellows who run along with him. The devil-dancer, seeing the frightened condition of his companions, turns his back to them, and throws some balls of rice into his mouth, and some on the ground, and then returns to the devil-temple. Here all the congregation are lying prostrate before the images, with closed eyes, lest they should be killed by their devil-gods, who are supposed to have gone to the cremation-ground to receive the bloody offerings. When the devil-dancer comes in they all rise and stand on their feet; then he distributes to them the sacred ashes and flowers, and the remaining part of the night is spent in dancing and singing in praise of the devils, by the devil-dancers. On the following morning several rams are slain as a sacrifice to the devils, and after this the people disperse to their respective homes.

The devil-dancers make an income from the villagers. Whenever they come to pay their vows and offerings to the demi-gods, the devil-dancers extract a good deal from them. Sometimes they play the part of sorcerers and fortune-tellers among the most ignorant classes; sometimes they act as devil-drivers, and on such occasions they receive a cock, some measures of rice, cocoanuts, fruits, and money. The devil-dancer knows how to further his own interests. If he sees anybody sick in the village, he tells that person that a little devil is the cause of the sickness, and he attempts to give a history of the devil which has got hold of that sick person. Immediately the sick person requests the devil-dancer to drive out the devil. In such ways he obtains an income sufficient to keep himself and his family alive. Some of these men have been known to grow rich by frightening the people, and threatening them with the anger, displeasure, and cruelty of the devils.

Some of the devil-dancers of the Indian villages have, in late years, left their old occupation, and embraced the ennobling and reforming religion of Jesus Christ. Among these men there is one who is well known to us, and whose character and later career are in every way remarkable. In the year 1877 there was a great famine in South India, and during this time of strain many poor villagers embraced Christianity. It is not for us to discuss the merit or demerit of their conversions. There was one among them who was a famous devil-dancer, and he knew all the tricks of the trade, and had never been backward in performing the tricks. When he was told of a religion which could make even a devil-dancer a good man, and that this religion destroys the works of the devil, and helps those who believe in it to lead a profitable and happy life under all circumstances, he readily embraced it, along with several other villagers; and he gave away to the missionary all his devil-dancer's dress, and the articles which he had used during his dark days. The famine passed, and plenty and prosperity re-visited the land, and then many of the villagers who embraced Christianity went back to their old religion, but this devil-dancer was not among them. He too well understood the emptiness and the falsehood of the religion which he had once professed. In refusing to go back to his old profession of a devil-dancer, and following his conviction in relation to the new religion, he lost a good living. Poor Joseph! Although he is a loser in one sense, he keeps a pure mind, a clear conscience, a happy soul, and a sound body, and he works hard as a gardener to support himself and his family. He is the only Christian man in his village. He does not work on Sundays, and he goes five miles every Sunday to attend a Christian service. We have recorded this fact here because we know the man personally; we spoke to him when he was a devil-dancer; we prayed with him for his conversion; we rejoiced with him after his conversion; and we make inquiries concerning him whenever we see a man from his village. We take a deep interest in him, as he is not only a fellow Christian but also a native of our own birth-place. We hope that the time will soon arrive when the devil-dancers of the villages will become worshippers of the one and holy God, in spirit and in truth.

8. THE FORTUNE-TELLER (Astrologer).

If there is a land under the sun where men believe thoroughly in astrology and fortune-telling, that land is India. It is no matter of surprise, therefore, to find that the villagers of India support their own sooth-sayers and fortune-tellers, who give vain hopes, and bring unnecessary trouble upon the much-burdened villagers. As a matter of fact, these fortune-tellers dupe the ignorant people with all kinds of tomfoolery and deception. The men and women of the village are easily led by the nose by these astrologers. The young and the old, the rich and the poor, the men and the women, always have something concerning which they wish to consult either an astrologer or a fortune-teller. When a man or woman, a cow or a buffalo, a goat or a sheep is sick, the first thing the head of the house does is to consult the fortune teller, asking him to reveal the cause of the sickness of the person or the beast. For this he pays a fee to the fortune-teller, as well as fruits, cocoanuts, etc. The villagers have a crude notion that all sickness, and all the difficulties in life, are caused by their family goddess, or through the schemes of some devil who is offended by their behaviour towards him.

There are several kinds of astrologers and fortune-tellers in the villages. Some of the Brahmin priests play this part. The *Vallavars* (the pariah priests) and men from other classes also become astrologers. These wise men write *sathagam* (horoscopes) for all classes and conditions of people who are able to pay for them. In this *sathagam* very singular things are mentioned. Take, for instance, the horoscope of Raman, a villager. In it we find described several things that Raman will do during his lifetime. All the enjoyments, sorrows, losses, gains, sicknesses, and changes in his life are mentioned in it. It seems that Raman will have several children between the twenty-fifth and thirty-fifth years of his age; he will have four male children and three female children. Out of these five will live to grow up, and the rest will die young. Between Raman's forty-second and forty-fifth years one of his parents, or both, will die. Raman himself will have serious sicknesses at the ages of twenty-five, thirty, thirty-five, forty-two, forty-eight, and fifty-five. At all these different periods of sickness he may possibly die. If he escapes the serious illness of fifty-five, then he will live up to threescore and ten. Between the ages of twenty-five and thirty-five a good star will be guiding our friend Raman. From the year thirty-five to forty-five Raman will have a bad star to guide him, and this will mean loss of property and possibly life. Then again Raman will have the influence of a good star, and this will bring him additional property and joy.

Without proceeding further on this subject, we may remark that the obtaining of these horoscopes has done much more harm than good. Consulting this horoscope at the time of sickness tends to bring fears which retard recovery. In times of trouble the horoscope creates doubts, and induces carelessness, and so kills one's spirit. In times of prosperity and happiness it foretells the miseries and troubles that are to follow, and so it acts the part of an enemy to human happiness.

No marriage among any class of the people can take place without consulting the horoscopes of both the man and the woman. This consultation often prevents good matches, and may even encourage unsuitable matrimonial transactions. In relation to the superstitious belief of the Hindus, there is a story current which runs thus:

There was a celebrated king in the city of Nagapore some hundreds of years ago. There was also a famous astrologer who was in the habit of visiting the palace of the king. On a certain occasion, 'How long shall I live?' was the question put to the astrologer by the king. Having carefully examined the horoscope, 'Only two years; not more,' replied the astrologer. The king's mind became troubled, his countenance was changed, and he became sorrowful and uneasy. But the Prime Minister, who was near him, suddenly called the astrologer, and said to him, 'How long will *you* live, let me know?' 'Ah, twenty years yet,' said the astrologer. At once the Prime Minister drew his sword and cut off the head of the astrologer. Then he addressed the king thus: 'How was it possible for a man who did not know the time of his own death, though it was so nigh, to predict that the death of your highness will take place in two years' time? Therefore, O king! take courage; believe not in superstitious men.' The king was comforted, and became as happy as before. Although this is a current story among the villagers, they do not practise what it teaches.

Not only is the consulting of astrologers and the taking of horoscopes an evil among the Hindus: it is also believed in and practised by the Mohammedan rulers. The famous and cruel Tippoo, Sultan of Mysore, consulted the astrologers in the year 1799 A.D., when his kingdom was falling, but nothing helped him to avert its ruin, or to save him from the hands of the conquering British.

There is a class of fortune-tellers called *Kodangee*, who travel about from village to village and tax the people for telling their fortunes. These men have a long pipe in their hands, and adorn themselves with ear-rings, finger-rings, and bangles; but, as a rule, they are men who cannot read or write their own language, though they show that they are possessed by a goddess named Sakkamadavi, who reveals to them the unknown future. They go to every house in the village, and if anyone has any particular thing he or she desires, he pays the man a measureful of grain, or a penny or two, who at once takes his long pipe and blows on it for a few minutes. In blowing this pipe there is no very charming musical sound to be heard, but he pretends to call out to his goddess by this means, and ask her to reveal this secret to him. Then he mutters a few words carrying a double meaning, and then he blows his pipe for a minute or two more, and so he goes on until he gets some clue to an answer from the people themselves. If a villager has lost his cow, and wants to find out its whereabouts, he consults this fortune-teller. As soon as he has blown his pipe, he reveals the secret to the villager that he was very seriously thinking about some *human being*. If the villager is quiet and serious in his attitude, the fortune-teller goes on to say that he was thinking of the marriage of his daughter, and so his goddess revealed to him that a fine and suitable husband would come from the northern direction to marry his daughter. In some cases the fortune-teller will talk to a villager, and get out of him all the secrets of each house, and then go to the other houses, easily telling everybody their fortunes.

There are some people who practise palmistry in the villages. They do not go, as a rule, from village to village, but the people who want to have their palms read go to the special man, and get their fortunes told or written by him. For this they have to pay a fee of from four to five shillings. Some of the villagers keep the written 'fortune' in their houses, and refer to it as often as they can. We cannot say anything as to the truth or error of palmistry as a science. There are people in the Western countries who believe in it, though it has not gained the approval of recognised scientific men.

There is another class of fortune-tellers called *Kurigar*, who are a set of women of the Koravar caste. These *Kurigars* are entirely ignorant people, but somehow they have the knack of getting at the female portion of the villagers, and they pretend to reveal the fortunes which are in store for them, and of course extract something from them in return. They carry with them a basket and a cane. With the cane they touch the hands of the women as they go on telling their fortunes. These fortune-tellers are considered out-caste people, and therefore they cannot touch the women of the higher castes of the village. The young unmarried women of the villages try to get into the good graces of these *Kurigars* by giving them some measures of grain or some money. Their object is to find out the temper, beauty, position, and parentage of their future husband, and some of them even try to ascertain the time of their marriage. Poor creatures! This evil is due to the custom of not allowing these girls to choose husbands according to their own preferences.

There is yet another class of fortune-tellers, who beat a drum while they tell fortunes. These men give out that they are possessed by a devil, who reveals to them the mysteries of the world. These are very boisterous and noisy men; they frighten their clients with their loud voices and excited gestures. These fortune-tellers find a suitable sphere among the most ignorant and the lowest caste people.

There is another kind of fortune-teller, who frequently visits the villages at midnight, rattling away his small drums, and calling on *Sakkamadavi* and *Ombathoo-Kambalam*, *i.e.*, his goddess and his departed ancestors. When the people hear his voice they open the door and place a measure or half a measure of grain on a fan outside the door. The fortune-teller takes the grain and leaves the fan behind. As soon as he approaches a house he says, 'Jayam varudoo, jayam varudoo,' *i.e.*, 'Success is coming to this house.' If the inmates of the house do not give him any grain, the blessing will be reversed on the following night, and the fortune-teller emphasizes the words, 'Aba jayam varudoo, aba jayam varudoo,' *i.e.*, 'Disaster is coming! disaster is coming!' Most of the villagers fear these fortune-tellers much, and dread greatly getting a curse from them.

IV.

PUBLIC LIFE.

1. THE MAGISTRATE (*Munsif*).

The office of village *munsif* may be compared to that of a mayor, or a justice of the peace, in a town or large village in Western countries. He is not elected by the people, as he sometimes is in the West, but he is appointed by the Government, and paid a monthly salary of rupees, five to twelve, according to the nature of the village of which he is put in charge. This salary is paid from the 'village service fund.' The village *munsif* is generally a man of some position, and his office is hereditary. He is the head officer of the village, and he has magisterial and judicial powers. As a magistrate, he punishes persons for petty assaults and offences; and as a judge he tries suits for sums of money, or other personal property, up to the value of ten rupees; and there is no appeal against his decision. If parties agree, he calls a *panchayet* (court of arbitration), which can adjudicate suits up to the value of one hundred rupees.

Most of the village *munsifs* are ignorant men who do not understand what justice means, or what the law of the land is. For all that, the *munsif* knows that he is justice of the peace, and he does not hesitate to deal with the villagers just as he may please.

We have no grudge against any village *munsif*, or any

other village officer, but we are compelled to speak the truth in the interests of the millions of India.

The corruption and fraud of the subordinate native village officers are not known either to the Government or to their superior officers. A village is too often a hot-bed of trouble, and a place of tyranny and wickedness. In comparing the village accountant with the village *munsif*, the former must be regarded as better than the latter, because he has no judicial or magisterial power. Both are sworn robbers, students of one school, and 'birds of the same feather.' Indeed, they are a great curse to the village. The *munsif* will sell a man for a farthing, and kill a man for a penny. Everyone in the village fears this monster, not because of the office he holds, but because of the evil which he is able to work. In view of the mischief which can be done to the villagers by this officer, we cannot help saying that he is an unnecessary evil, and that the present staff of men ought to be deposed, and a new set of men, with better training and better supervision, ought to be appointed in their places. The collectors and *tahsildars* of districts and the police officers should have their eye upon them. The hereditary nature of these offices ought certainly to be abolished. In fact, there ought to be a strict and immediate check over village *munsifs*. Not till then will the peace of the Indian villages be secured.

What is said elsewhere of a village accountant may be said also of a village *munsif*. He often abuses his authority and becomes a great source of discomfort, inconvenience and trouble to the villagers. What famine, pestilence and war are to a nation a village *munsif* is to the poor Indian villagers. How many crimes are hushed up by receiving bribes from the offenders! How many innocent people are sentenced to rigorous imprisonment, and how many innocent people are hanged by the neck! How many innocent people are sent to the penal colonies, as life prisoners, by the false reports of this reckless village officer! And how many homes are destroyed by his jealousy and ill-will!

By the assertion of his authority he gets milk daily, free of charge, from one villager; pulse, grain and vegetables from another; lambs and rams from some poor shepherd; and firewood is supplied even by the poor pariahs. On ceremonial days he gets oil from the oilmonger, flowers from the flower-sellers, and straw and hay for his cattle, and even makes the poor villagers plough and work in his fields for him as a tribute to his honour.

2. THE COURT OF ARBITRATION.

In almost every village disputes are settled by the *panchayet*, or court of arbitration. Without involving themselves in any serious costs, the village folk have settled disputes of all kinds for centuries at these courts. There are two kinds of *panchayets*. One is called the *jatheekoottam*, *i.e.*, the *panchayet* of different castes. This court may consist of five, ten, twenty, thirty, fifty, or a hundred. The other court of arbitration is called the village *panchayet*, and consists of five members only. The members of this *panchayet* are elected by the villagers themselves, and they may belong to any class save the lowest order. They receive no payment whatever from the villagers. They are generally men of position who enjoy the confidence of the villagers.

In each village there is a place called *Madam* (village inn), which is used as the court of the *panchayet*. The court sits at 8 p.m., after the judges have taken their supper. They order the watchman of the village to bring the parties who have disputes before them. The eldest of the members of the *panchayet* becomes the chief judge of the court, and he receives money from the parties as security. When the case is decided, he returns the money to them.

The *panchayet* decides suits of all kinds, such as land disputes, petty quarrels, divorce, division of property, debts, temple disputes, disputes between the barber and the villagers, the washerman and the villagers, disputes between the artizan classes and the villagers. If they find any of the villagers become disobedient and troublesome to the *panchayet*, they unanimously adopt the plan of letting him be an isolated man in the village. No villager is allowed to speak to him, or to exchange fire, or any other necessary with him. In former times he was even forbidden to take water from the public well.

The manner in which the *panchayet* inquires into the case is very interesting. If there is moonlight, they keep no lamp in the court-house, but they make use of the 'poor man's lantern.' During other nights they light the lamp belonging to the inn. This lamp is made out of stone, and kept in a corner. It is filled with lamp-oil, and a piece of thread is put in it, which is lighted. The light is very dim, and only just enough to allow the people to see that there is a lamp in the corner. The judges, the parties in the suit, and the spectators are alike indifferent about light, because there is nothing to be transacted in writing, except the *muchilika*, *i.e.*, the agreement, and this is drawn up during the daytime.

When the court is opened, the watchman of the village

calls out for the parties to appear. The plaintiff is first summoned. When he enters the court-house he prostrates himself before the judges. 'Get up,' says the chief judge. When the man gets up he states his complaint. If all the parties are present, the judges go through the case, otherwise they postpone it until the following week. On hearing the complaints of the plaintiff in a petty quarrel, the judges ask him to bring his evidences. Then they hear the statements of the defendant and his witnesses. Before they sum up the case, and give their judgment, they ask all those present in the inn to retire, and then they talk about the matter for some hours among themselves. When they have arrived at a conclusion, they call the parties to come in, and the chief judge delivers the judgment. If the judges find the accused to be guilty of the charge brought against him, he receives the following judgment: 'Thou fool! bad donkey! pariah dog! Have not you got any work to do? How dare you assault the woman who has brought this charge against you? Beware! beware, you donkey! we charge you, in the name of our village goddess Kali, to bring ten cocoanuts as a sacrifice for the sins referred to in this case, and, besides this, you will give three rupees to the village fund as a fine.' On hearing the judgment delivered by the chief, the offender prostrates himself before the judges, saying, 'You must forgive me this time; you must forgive me this time.' Of course, this is the form of appeal he makes against their decision. If any one of the judges thinks that the man is not in very good circumstances, he whispers to the other judges to reduce the sentence; if not, they insist upon the man paying the fine, and breaking the cocoanuts to the goddess.

All other cases are tried by them in a similar manner. This system of *panchayet* is very convenient, and it is not expensive for the poor villagers; but we are sorry to say that this system is not much in use at present, since the Indian Bar is overcrowded by lawyers in all the cities and towns, and these are a great drain on the poor ryots of India. They induce the villagers to go to the regular courts for every imaginable thing, and there they suck the blood out of them. If the Government of India would only encourage the *panchayet* system, the mass of the people would be greatly benefited, and the wicked village *munsifs*, and the rascally village accountants, and the wily lawyers, would not be so well able to disturb the peace of the village.

The *panchayet* of the Marava class was held under the shade of a large tamarind-tree near a village named Karisa Kalam, in the Madura district. When we were in our lodging we heard one day the voice of the Indian trumpet, about 8 a.m., for clan *panchayets* are held during the daytime, as well as in the night. The people who came from different villages heard the noise of the trumpet, and assembled under the tree. It was quite an imposing sight, for there were crowds of men of different ages and positions. They all sat down on the ground under the tree. They had appointed a man to keep the accounts, and to register the names of the parties in the villages who had disputes to be settled. There were only five men to settle all the disputes. The cases came on, one after the other. A wife brought a charge against her husband; a father brought a charge against a son, and the son brought an answering charge against the father; one brother brought a charge against another brother; a stepmother brought a charge against a stepson. There were also land disputes and property disputes. All these disputes were amicably settled. They excused some parties, punished some, and reconciled some. All this was done in good order, without the slightest confusion or irregularity, and with much saving of time and expense to the people.

In the district of Tinnevelly we were present at a similar kind of meeting of this class, but the court was then assembled in the night, about 8 p.m., when all the parties concerned had returned from their day's work. It was quite a large meeting. All the parties assembled in the centre of the village, in the moonlight. Of course, we were there as visitors. The chief of the court began the sitting by distributing betel-nut, sandal-wood and flowers to all that were present. These things are purchased from the funds collected in the way of fines. There were two cases heard that night. In the one case, a young man brought a charge against his wife, and in the other a boy brought a charge against his father. Both of these cases were exceedingly interesting, and even amusing. In the former case, the young man accused his wife of unfaithfulness. The young man, when only eighteen years, had gone to a certain wedding of some relatives. His wife, who, it appears, was then twenty-five years of age, had gone to that same wedding, and there the two first saw each other, and fell in love. They fixed the day for their marriage without seeking the consent of their parents or other relatives. Three months after their marriage the woman began to sleep in her sister's house, having left her husband to sleep in his own house. The man advised her, scolded her, and even beat her, but all in vain—she persisted in sleeping in her sister's house. And this gave him room to suspect her conduct. The woman, in her statement, mentioned that her husband was quite a boy, who did not know how to manage a wife, and he was playful and stupid, and did not earn enough to support her. Besides this, every meal that was prepared in the house was consumed by her husband, leaving her hardly anything to live upon, and therefore she was compelled to go to her sister's home and get some food. The wise judges, after hearing the statements of both sides, advised them to forgive each other, and to lead a peaceful life.

In the latter case, the boy brought a charge against his father for marrying another woman and leaving him and his mother without proper support. The judges, on hearing both sides, decided that the father of the boy should give maintenance to both his wife and his son.

3. LAWSUITS.

Ignorance and lawlessness usually go together, and a singular love for lawsuits is characteristic of the less civilized Indian people. It is an admitted fact that one of the principal causes of the poverty of the people is this fondness for litigation.

There are always some men in every village who are engaged in a lawsuit of some kind, either civil or criminal. There is sure to be some case pending in the *Taluk* Court, or in the Deputy Collector's Office, or in the *Munsif's* Court, or in the District Court, or in the District Collector's Office. There are cases that hang on for months together in the High Court, at the Revenue Board, or in the Governor's Office; and there are appeals waiting for decision even in the English Privy Council. Both the plaintiff and the defendant have plausible reasons for affirming that they have a good case to fight out; and their advocates are still more clever in exaggerating the importance of the cases. Each party has this assurance from his own legal adviser; and these men annually take a large share of the villagers' hard-earned money, with which they build fashionable houses in the cities and towns, and purchase the best of properties in the country.

The contentions which induce the ryots to squander their money in litigation often arise out of very simple things. If two brothers fall out about some trivial matter, one of them will take a plough, and turn over the soil a cubit beyond his proper line of demarcation. This wilful action of the elder brother, Ramsing, is quite enough to annoy his younger brother, Gopalsing. A dispute consequently arises over this piece of land, which is not worth more than five shillings Gopalsing starts at once to arrange for the settlement of the dispute in court. Of course, Ramsing is quite willing to stand against his brother. Both go to some legal adviser, and get his opinion on the merits of their case. Both seem to have good grounds for their action, and both have sufficient witnesses and documents at hand. Gopalsing has engaged an able lawyer of the town — at least, so he thinks; and he pays him a sum of £10 as lawyer's fees, and £3 as out-fees, promising a further sum of £20 if he wins the case. The shrewd lawyer assures Gopalsing that his is undoubtedly a 'winning case,' and that he has never met with a case so good and clear as his. These kind words of the lawyer cheer his spirits, and he returns home in a hopeful frame of mind. On his arrival in the village, he publishes among his friends what his lawyer has told him, and he feels quite sanguine of his success. In the meantime Ramsing has got hold of a leading barrister, and has paid him a good sum of money as his fee. This barrister assures Ramsing that his opponent, Gopalsing, has no case at all, and that it is very foolish of him to attempt to fight the case in the court. But he asks Ramsing to see him on the following morning. Ramsing gets up very early the next morning, and hurries up to the lawyer's house, and the lawyer gets his clerk to read the answers which he has written on the plaint. As soon as Ramsing hears the answers he leaps for joy. 'Would you like to have any more answers?' politely asks the learned counsel. 'No, sir; there are plenty,' replies Ramsing. 'All right—you can go; I shall attend to the matter,' says the lawyer. Fortunately, Ramsing had dreamed a dream during the previous night which indicated his success, and this, together with the lawyer's words, redoubles the joy of Ramsing, who boldly gives out through the village that he is certain to succeed. The suit is filed in the Lower Court. There are many postponements of the case, and on all these occasions both of the parties, and all their witnesses, have to go up from their village to the town, which may be twenty or thirty miles distant, spending, of course, a considerable sum of money in travelling and food.

At last the day for hearing the case arrives. The parties are all present, the witnesses are heard, the documents are examined, and the counsel for each party pleads his cause well. Then the judge, having weighed the evidence, gives his judgment, perhaps, in favour of Gopalsing. Ramsing's counsel at once puts the blame of the result entirely upon the carelessness of the judge, and makes his own uncharitable remarks about him. However, he is quite sure that the judgment will be reversed on appeal, and he induces Ramsing to make the appeal at once. That means another expenditure of twenty to thirty pounds, which his client brings readily enough and gives to him. The lawyer appeals to the District Court against the decision of the Lower Court, and perhaps wins his case after some months of waiting. The tables are now turned on Gopalsing, who, nothing daunted, goes to the High Court in Bombay, where there are so many *vakils*, barristers, advocates, and attorneys-at-law. These men, who are working at the highest court of the presidency, are supposed to be great men, who cannot take cases for the same fee that Gopalsing has paid for counsel at the Lower Court. Their demand is at least double or treble fees. Gopal has to lay out some fifty pounds for lawyer's fees, and about fifteen pounds as out-fees. Ramsing also engages a barrister to watch his interest in this highest court. After much anxiety and delay, the High Court Judges confirm the decision of the District Court—Gopalsing has lost his case, and Ramsing has won it; but both of them are serious losers. They have spent more than a hundred pounds each over a piece of land which is not worth more than five shillings. And to their money losses must be added their loss of working time in the three years during which they have been wandering about, speaking and thinking and planning in connection with the case. This is but one instance out of a thousand which are constantly occurring.

That justice is only to be bought at a ruinous cost is a fact that cannot be denied. The stamp fees, the court fees, the lawyers' fees, travelling expenses and other out-fees, all help to bring to ruin the villager who enters into litigation. His health is broken, some of his lands have to be mortgaged, the fields are left without proper cultivation, and he gets into the clutches of the money-lenders. All this is the consequence of his giving way to his passion, neglecting the village *panchayet* and favouring the law-courts. There are ninety cases out of every hundred which could be easily and amicably settled among the villagers themselves, without incurring any loss of money or time for the villagers, if they only had better sense and understood 'the art of living peaceably together.'

One of the chief reasons for the villagers getting mixed up in lawsuits is the craftiness, wickedness, foolishness, and rascality of the village officers, who are better known to the public under the designations of village *munshees* and village accountants. These two public officers, instead of maintaining peace in the villages, get up false cases to bring the villagers into trouble and to destroy their peace and prosperity. In all the lawsuits of the villagers these two officers come out as witnesses, either on the plaintiff's side or on the defendant's. The higher authorities generally believe the evidence of these men, because they are public and responsible officers; but we know that they often come to the public courts and utter shameless falsehoods in giving their evidence. The less their evidence is believed, the better it is for all the parties concerned.

English legal terms are used among the villagers in a very corrupted and diverted form. The word 'rule' is used, and pronounced among the villagers as *nool*, meaning 'thread'; the word 'acts' as *âgattoo*, meaning 'yes.' The word 'subpœna' is used as *subbanna*, the name of a person. The term 'evidence act' is used *yavadometoo kāttoo*, meaning 'asking the whereabouts'; the word 'issue' as *Yāsoo*, meaning 'Jesus'; the word 'hearing' as *eerankee*, meaning 'having come down'; the word 'statement' as *sattoometto;* the word 'cross' as *keerâo*—and a host of other words are confusedly or oddly used.

4. THE WATCHMAN (*Kavalkar*).

It is proverbial that India is a country full of villages. Every village is isolated in itself. The inhabitants of the villages are of different castes, and therefore, when there is public danger to their persons or their property, they are quite unable to present a united front. There are always some persons in every village who are in the habit of stealing petty things, such as fruits, vegetables, cocoanuts, cotton, straw, plantain-leaves, flowers, and even cattle and fowls. House-breaking, highway robbery, and dacoity are also common in the villages. To prevent such crimes the villagers employ one or more *kavalkars*, or watchmen. Their duty is to protect the life and property of the villagers. In the Tinnevelly and Madura Districts this *kaval* occupation has fallen into the hands of a class of people known as *maravars*, who are a brave and warlike people, and whose forefathers were the founders of the Pandian and Chola dynasties of South India. The strength and valour of this class gave them a pre-eminence in the kingdoms of the different Hindu and Moghul monarchs of past times. A history of this class has been written by the author of the present work, under this title, 'The Ancient Heroes of the South Indian Peninsula.' A study of this will enlighten our readers concerning this peculiar race. Other classes of people are also employed as village *kavalkars*. This village police force does not wear any uniform, but each of its members holds a rod of office. They receive no monthly payments from the villagers, but they have an annual income from each house in the shape of both grain and money. Besides this, the gardeners will occasionally oblige them with presents of vegetables. During the festivals they get a certain sum of money and gifts. This income is divided among the *kavalkars*, if there are many of them.

There is a *kaval* system known as *sthalam kaval—i.e.*, protection of districts. A certain influential and well-to-do man takes the *kaval* (watch) of several villages together, and then he appoints his own men in each village to do the work of the *kavalkar*, and he pays them a certain sum when they have collected all the contributions of the villagers and brought them to him. This moving spirit is called *thalamaykar—i.e.*, 'the headman.'

The village watchman goes round the village several times during the night with his staff in his hand, which is from ten to eleven feet long. A blow from this club will almost be a death-blow. Some of these watchmen go to the corn-fields in the night to prevent the crops from being stolen. During the day the watchmen attend to the work of the village, and they wait for the orders of the *panchayet*, the village accountant, and the village *munsif*. They also help in collecting the taxes.

If any of the villagers prove unfriendly to a watchman, or refuse to pay his wages, the watchman will teach him a lesson. All of a sudden he will go to the man who refuses to pay his wages, and tell him a story of this kind—that he has lost a fine and beautiful hen from his yard, and that he saw the footprint of a big jackal which had doubtless done the mischief. The simple-minded villager will sympathize with the poor watchman. Then the watchman spreads the news of his loss about amongst the villagers. Having done this, he allows a day or two to pass by, and then he himself plays the part of a jackal by stealing a fowl from the very man who has refused to keep the usual terms with him. If the man who has lost his fowl complains to the watchman, he has his answer ready. He at once reminds him of the fowl that he himself lost, and assures him that he saw the jackal coming from the jungle in the night. 'Ah yes, I will watch and catch the jackal rascal within a night or two; but will you kindly pay up my arrears,' says this honourable watchman. If this does not induce the villager to settle the account, the watchman goes a step further. He takes his comrades, and goes to the fields of the villager, and they help themselves to the ears of corn, and return home in the dead of night. In the morning the villager is aroused by this very watchman, and told that his field has been robbed, and on inquiry he finds that an enemy has done it. 'However,' continues the watchman, 'I am not going to leave the robber so easily, but I should be glad if you would settle my account.' If the villager is still indifferent about paying up the arrears, he has to learn a further lesson. The watchman arranges with his friends, and steals one of the beasts of the villager, and sends it off a hundred miles away, and then waits patiently to enjoy the fun. When the villager reports the loss of his beast, the watchman is the first man to suggest to him that he ought to have recourse to witchcraft. 'I know a person in the village of Peryakoolam, fifty miles distant, who is clever in giving a clue which will help you to find the cattle-robbers. If you want me to, I shall be happy to go up there and bring him back; but please settle my account,' says the watchman. If the villager agrees to settle the account of the watchman, well and good; if not, the watchman plans a house-breaking or a dacoity. In the latter case he works so well as to bring men from a distant place to teach a lesson to the hard-hearted, self-willed, and miserly villager. When all the people have retired to their beds, a gang of robbers, with torchlights, clubs, knives, swords, slings, and other weapons, surround the house of the villager. The watchman, with his staff, goes to every house in the village and awakes the people, calling upon them to come out and help him in defending the person and the property of the villager, named, perhaps, Balu. But none of the villagers have the courage to follow the watchman. By the time the watchman has informed all the villagers of the attack, by going from house to house, half of Balu's property has been seized by the robbers, and some of the members of Balu's family have been wounded, especially if they have offered any resistance. At last the watchman and a few of the more courageous villagers come to the spot, to save Balu and his property, but they find the house surrounded by armed men of undaunted courage and valour. To satisfy the villagers, the watchman takes his big stick, and rushes at the gang, saying, '*Rodoo, podoo!* (Strike, strike!) Where have you come, you robbers? I will kill you all at one blow of my club. Why will you die? Get back, get back; run away, run away!' This is the voice of the watchman while he is rushing at the gang. He twirls his stick about, and tries to beat some of the robbers; but he gets it back from the robbers, and soon the blood rushes from his head and from the wounds in his legs and hands. Down he falls, and lies speechless and motionless, until the robbers have had time to clear away from the village.

The institution of the village watchman is somewhat peculiar. His work is hereditary, and he has no source of income for his maintenance besides his office, so that he is dependent upon the villagers for his support. His work does not give him time to do any additional jobs, and as a rule, he is not fitted for doing anything else. Hence, he adopts these wicked methods for compelling the villagers to give him his annual allowances. We cannot approve of the watchman's schemes for securing his wages from the villager, but neither can we approve of the wilful stubbornness of the villager, who shirks his duty in not supporting the man who is appointed to protect his life and property.

The Government of India has not put a stop altogether to the village dacoity, but it is not now what it once was. It is a great advantage to the villagers to keep the watchman regularly paid his allowance, and to treat him in a proper manner. For the watchman is responsible for any theft that takes place, and he ought to pay the cost of the lost property out of his own pocket. And while this is the rule, it is manifestly improper for the villager to quarrel with the watchman, or to become irregular in paying his appointed wages.

5. THE ACCOUNTANT (*Karnam*).

The *karnam*, or village accountant, generally belongs to the caste known as Vellalas. He is an important revenue officer, and has several important duties to discharge. He has to collect the land taxes of all kinds from the villagers. He confines his work to one village if it provides a sufficient income; if not, he adds the accountantship of one or two other villages. The office is hereditary. No one has a right to be appointed a village accountant who does not belong to the family of some revenue officer. They are intelligent and crafty and clever at figures. They always carry about with them a knife and an iron pen (a long piece of iron, in the shape of a large needle, attached to the knife). With this pen they write on palm-leaves.

In the villages which belong to the Government, the accountant is under the authority of the higher revenue officers. In the villages which belong to Zamindars or other proprietors, the accountant is under their orders; but they have no power to dismiss him from his office. All they can do is to bring a charge against him before the district judge, and he, after careful investigation, may dismiss the accountant, and appoint in his stead one of the accountant's family who may be eligible for the office.

The accountants who are under the direct control of the Government receive a fixed monthly salary, varying from 7 to 12 rupees, according to the amount of work they have to do. In the Zamindari villages the accountant has endowments of lands, the revenue of which goes towards his support. And this is not all; every village accountant can demand from each villager a certain quantity of grain at the time of harvest. Besides this, he gets from them a considerable supply of vegetables, fruits, and other produce. The accountant is always bent upon making money by fair means or foul. In every dispute and quarrel of the villagers the accountant has a hand. He has power to do and undo things in the village. He thinks that to allow a village to be in peace is to injure his own interests. So 'Divide, and rule, and gain,' is his motto. A careful investigation will lead to the conclusion that the accountant is at the bottom of almost all the troubles and difficulties rising in the villages.

In treating of the dishonesty and tyranny of the accountant, it is difficult to know where to begin and where to end. When we see him writing the village accounts, we find that he is a man of business, tact, shrewdness, and ability. It is truly said that 'an accountant should swallow the accounts, or the accounts will swallow the accountant,' but in writing the accounts he is really scheming to destroy the social and domestic happiness of some of the villagers. It must be remembered that most of the villagers are so ignorant as not to be able to read and write their own vernacular language. Hence the accountant plays the part of teacher, lawyer, philosopher, guide, and rogue. The great time of harvest for the wily accountant is the distribution of annual *pattaw*. Every landowner of the village must give something to the accountant when he receives the *pattaw*. There are villagers who have failed to give their offerings to their family gods; there are villagers who have failed to keep their vows to the demons. But this bloodsucker of the village—the accountant—will leave no one without getting some harvest from him. If a man fails to get the money, the accountant will put off giving his *pattaw*, and make him wander up and down, or else he will make some wilful mistakes in the *pattaw*. And he will go so far even as to give one man's *pattaw* to another, and thus he will make a delightful muddle.

The accountant is noted for his document-writing, for he is the only man who is able to write with pen and ink in the village. He gets money for every document he writes. Besides this, he will write false documents, in order to bring his enemy or his friends' enemy into trouble. Suppose that Gopal is an enemy of a village accountant. The accountant writes a false document, and says it has been executed by Gopal to Raman, the friend of the accountant, for 500 rupees, which have been borrowed by the former from the latter. The accountant knows that Gopal can only make his mark —he cannot sign his name. The accountant, having strengthened the document with some false witnesses, gets his friend to file the suit in due time in the Court of the Subordinate Judge. He keeps Gopal in entire ignorance of what he is doing. When the summons is issued by the court, calling on Gopal to pay 500 rupees, he faints and drops down; his wife beats her breast, rolls on the ground, and knocks her head against the wall; and his poor children, just returned from the field, cry without knowing what is the matter with their parents. And so there is a great commotion in the house of Gopal. The judge forms his opinion upon the facts before him. He has a respectable village accountant, who gives his evidence that he has written the document, and that Gopal received the 500 rupees in his presence; and there are other witnesses also. In the face of all this, the judge gives his judgment against Gopal, and Gopal is ruined, for his few acres of land, which were his only means of support, have to be sold.

In seeking for the reasons why Gopal has incurred the displeasure of the accountant, we come utterly to hate the wretch. Probably it is this: Gopal's wife refused to yield to the evil desires of this monster; or it may be that Gopal, being a poor man, refused to pay the unreasonable taxes that were demanded from him.

6. THE SAVINGS BANKS.

It is not an easy matter to find a large capitalist in a village community. The properties of the villagers are dry and wet lands for cultivation, cocoanut palm *topes*—*i.e.*, groups of trees—palmyra palm *topes*, and mango and plantain *topes*. But the currency of money among the villagers is a difficult thing at all times. Therefore, in order to have lump sums of money, they have wisely organized a system of village savings banks. The main object of this system is to clear the debts which they incur, and, if possible, to purchase more lands to meet the demands of their increasing families. The system of banking is this: An influential landlord opens a bank in a village, and he contributes 10 rupees a month, and also gets other twenty or thirty persons of the village to join this *chit*, as it is called. When all the parties have joined and contributed the first instalment, the bank-owner takes the money—say, 200 rupees—the contributions of twenty members during the first month, and he spends the money as he pleases. In the second month, nineteen names of the other members are written on small pieces of palm-leaves and cast before the members when they are assembled. A boy or a girl is commissioned to pick up one of these pieces, and hand it over to the banker, who announces the name to whose lot the second drawing has fallen. Then this person takes the money, after giving a proper security to the banker, who is responsible for all the money deposited by the members. In this way the bank lottery runs on every month, until the last man gets his 200 rupees. The advantage of joining this bank is the interest that a depositor gets on 200 rupees before he can deposit as much as 30 or 40 rupees. Those who receive the money by lottery before the tenth month is out, have a great gain, and those who receive afterwards have a less gain, but they get the money in a lump sum. This system of banking is called the *chit*. There is no clerk, no office, no paid establishment of any kind, in transacting this business, but the advantage to the banker is that he takes 200 rupees on the first drawing, which he lends out on interest, or takes to meet his own requirements.

There is another system of saving money. A landlord

opens a bank on the lines we have described, except that he takes ten or twenty per cent. out of the 200 rupees from the party who gets the money each month, and distributes it as compound interest. In this way the thing goes on till the end of the term. When the whole term is over, the banker again starts his bank with more or fewer members, according to circumstances.

There is yet another system of money-saving going on among the villagers. A wealthy and reliable landlord gets fifty members each to contribute 10 rupees a month, on the same principle as described above, but the term-money collected is not distributed by lottery, as in the other two cases. In the beginning of the month, the parties meet on a *pial* (veranda) of the banker's house, and bring the 500 rupees, and put it up to auction. None but the members can bid. Whoever bids the lowest rate is allowed to draw the money for that month, and this scene is repeated each month. The member who bids for the money at the lowest rate loses 100 to 200 rupees, as the case may be, out of the subscribed sum of 500 rupees. When he draws the 300 rupees from the banker, he gives him a document promising to pay the full amount of rupees. The money which is gained by the auction is distributed among the other members who have not taken any money in the bank auction. So this system gives a great profit to those who simply keep depositing their money till the term is over. It is also in a way helpful to those men who bid for the money at the auction in paying up some of their urgent debts which they have incurred either by law-suits or by family trouble.

The savings-banks are not only organized on the monthly system of depositing money, they are also constituted to meet bi-monthly, or quarterly, or three times a year, or even half-yearly. The latter system is called the *Poo chit*, *i.e.*, the system of saving money at the time of harvest. There are two rice crops in a year for those who have wet cultivation. Hence the system of saving their money half-yearly by one of the foregoing systems.

There are female bankers in every village, who are working on a small scale as the men do.

Although there are several defects in the present system of village banking, which cannot be approved by civilized nations, yet it is a great benefit to the poor villagers, who could not otherwise command a lump sum of money to meet their urgent needs.

V.

LEISURE HOURS.

1. AMUSEMENTS.

PROBABLY there is not a people on the face of the globe, whether rich or poor, civilized or uncivilized, white or black, that does not find time for recreation and amusement. There are differences in the nature of the amusements, but everywhere time is found for some kind of pleasure-taking. Civilized societies, as we know, purchase their pleasure at a great cost, but the barbarous and the semi-barbarous obtain theirs at very little cost. The influences of these relief-times are much the same in both cases. The town folk of India have their expensive amusements, and the village folk have their inexpensive ones.

The most important are the village dramas. These are performed during the summer months, when all the harvests are over, and all the hard work of the year is finished. Then the tillers of the soil have a good deal of time on their hands. At such times a dramatic company will come into a village. The most familiar and famous of these dramatic companies perform two important dramas, namely, the drama of 'Harishandra' and that of 'Markanda.' These stories are most familiar to all the villagers, and therefore they take great delight in seeing the performances, and hearing the stories told over and over again. The former one relates the history of a king Harishandra, who lost his kingdom because he persisted in maintaining the principles of truthfulness to the very end, and had to leave his throne, and render menial service, being separated from his queen, Chandramadi, and from his only son and heir, Logida. The queen and her son became domestic servants in a priest's house. While they were in the priest's house, the son was bitten by a snake, and died. The king, who was forced to take a watchman's position in the cremation ground of a town, cremated his child without knowing whose child it was, as the child was brought to him in the night. The story on the whole is most pathetic, and even heartrending. We have seen many men and women moved by a clever actor who performs the part of Chandramadi weeping over her child's death. There was one very famous man, Jagasami by name, who skilfully played the part of the Queen Chandramadi. He showed a great deal of originality in representing the story, and he composed some new airs for some of the pathetic parts. His sweet feminine voice and wonderful gestures had a charming effect upon his audience wherever he went, and he was really a celebrated man of his time.

The story concerning 'Markanda' is this: His parents were entreating Siva to bless them by giving them a male child. Siva appeared to them, and said that he would grant them a male child, and he should become an honourable, God-fearing, excellent, beautiful and cultured young man, but would die at the age of sixteen. Or, if they preferred, he would grant them a son who would be most wicked, irreligious, indifferent, and ugly-looking, but would live for a hundred years. 'Which of these blessings do you choose?' said Siva. The parents asked for the former. So the child was born, and he grew in knowledge, strength, and devotion to the gods. When he was fifteen years of age, his parents

A DAY OF JOY.

began to be very unhappy and sorrowful, in thinking of the fast approaching doom of their son. The sensible lad was curious enough to ask the cause of this unhappiness of his parents. They then told him the fact, that he, their only and dear son, could live only one year more with them, and that this had been revealed to them by Siva. On receiving this news, the lad became alarmed. However, he took courage, and made the necessary arrangements to go to a jungle, where a mighty river was flowing. As the time was drawing nigh for his death, as fixed by his creator, he hastened to that solitary place, leaving his home and his parents. There he commenced to pray to Siva most earnestly to grant him a few more years of usefulness, and not to take his life at the early age of sixteen. Nevertheless, as prearranged, the angel of death came to him riding on a he-buffalo, and shot at him several sharp and poisoned arrows of affliction and death. But the lad continued in his prayers to Siva, and his devotion was such that the arrows proved harmless. Then the angel of death, with all his strength, sent a host of arrows of fiery trials, but these did not in the least hurt the lad, nor was the angel able to disturb him from his devotion. Then the angel of death repeated his arrows of various kinds, but still all in vain. The angel of death grew furious, and approached the lad, and attempted to take his life with the sword; but then Siva appeared, drove away the angel of death, and extended the age of Markanda, who was to live on for ever as a young man of sixteen years old. These two popular dramas are ever fresh and attractive to the villagers.

In a suitable centre of a group of villages, the dramatic company open their performances by erecting a temporary shed. At about nine o'clock at night the open ground will be crowded by villagers of both sexes and grown-up children;

there will be a sea of heads. Some of them come from distant villages in their bullock-carts. There will be a few petty bazaars, full of eatables, betel nuts, tobacco and snuff; there will be scarcely any lights among the crowd; the few there are will be near the stage. The performances are usually arranged in moonlight. The drama will commence at about ten o'clock, and will continue till four in the morning. As usual in all Indian dramas, the buffoon or merry-maker will occupy an hour or so at the commencement, and will cause the people to roar with laughter by his innumerable comical and humorous sayings and gestures. When the play commences the people are very attentive and orderly. Of course, those that are inclined to sleep will find the drama has a soporific effect upon them. Generally the performance of one of these famous stories will be repeated for twenty to thirty days. At the close of every night's performance a large white cloth will be spread near the stage, and the people will be invited to contribute money, and they throw the money on to the white cloth, while the dramatic party sing some sweet songs with musical accompaniments. When a man or woman throws money on the cloth, the jester mentions the name of that person to the crowd three times in a loud voice. Some of these villagers like this honour, and repeat the act of throwing money on the cloth. The oftener they throw money, the more they are praised and cheered. When the whole story is finished, at the end of twenty or thirty days, the villagers collect some money among themselves, and give it to the dramatic company, who keep moving from centre to centre till the autumn begins. Some of the villagers are so enamoured as to follow the dramatic company to a distance of thirty to forty miles.

In some villages a set of young men join together to dance

and sing in the moonlight. They have a leader, who leads and trains them in singing and dancing. These young men commit to memory songs that are known as *kummies*. These *kummies* are descriptive accounts of the heroes of the past, and the famous works, the 'Ramayana' and the 'Bharatta,' are also arranged in *kummi* form; and these are frequently used in the village dances. The young men dress themselves in white cloths, and wear dyed turbans on their heads. They hold a handkerchief and a fan in their hands. They march through the streets singing and dancing, and the villagers watch them with great admiration. Sometimes they go to each house, and dance before the inmates. If the young men know that there are only some unmarried young women in the house, they sing and dance smartly. Every one will try to show that he is the cleverest of the lot, both in dancing and singing, so that he may win the affection of some girl in the house, and lead her to take him as her partner. This kind of dancers do not receive any money for their work; they simply amuse themselves and the villagers.

There are several other kinds of amusement, some of them of a vulgar character. Bull-fighting, cock-fighting, and ram-fighting are common.

The bull-fighting must not be regarded as like the familiar bull-fighting in Spain, or any other Western country. This fight is called *sallikattoo*, and takes place during the day. A large plain is chosen for the purpose, and the villagers collect money among themselves with which to meet the necessary expenditure. They send out invitations to the people of other villages, and inform them of the fixed day for the bull-fight. This news spreads abroad among all classes of the people, who come in numbers in bands and parties, both men and women, to the spot appointed. The people of the village who have arranged for the bull-fight erect temporary sheds at their own cost in order to accommodate their visitors. As it is a public meeting-place, the sellers of various articles flock to it with their different kinds of goods.

At about eight o'clock in the morning all assemble in the plain. Sometimes there are thousands of people met on such occasions. Several fighting bulls will be brought by villagers from different districts. The owner of each bull ties a new cloth round its neck. In some cases the owner puts money in a corner of the cloth. He takes the bull to the headman of the assembly, and bows his head to him. Then the headman inquires concerning the man's parentage and name, if he does not happen to know him. Then he asks the herald or crier to beat his drum three times loudly. This is a sign for the people to understand that a fighting bull will be let loose in the midst of the assembly. This is the signal also to the men who have come to fight the bull, and take the cloth and the money from its neck, that they must hold themselves in readiness. The owner of the bull takes him to the centre of the assembly, and there he lets him loose by warning the bull to take care of himself, and to make his way through the crowd to his shed. As soon as ever the bull is set free, ten or fifteen men come to the front of the assembly without either stick or knife, and they face the bull manfully. Some of the clever bulls defend themselves for hours together, hurting many of those men, and sometimes killing one or two; at last they escape from their hands and go home, leaping and frisking for joy. There are many bulls who are known to be great fighters, and who never allow anyone to take the cloths from their necks. Whoever takes the cloth is considered to be a hero. The bullocks are brought in to fight, one after another, the whole day through, and sometimes this terrible struggle between man and beast will be continued for two or three days. Some of the owners of the bulls offer a large sum of money to anyone who can arrest their bulls before the assembly. These beasts are very knowing and clever in their fighting; they stand quietly before the assembly, and do not run or jump; but if anyone approaches them, they hit him with their horns or legs as quickly as a flash of lightning.

The people who come to witness the fight occupy the ground for half a mile in a crescent form. Some will sit and some will stand, just as they may please, and most of them will be exposed to the wind and the sun; but this they consider as nothing compared with the pleasure they derive from watching the bull-fight. The public do not pay a farthing on occasions of this kind.

Another amusement is the inhuman and barbarous habit of cock-fighting, and this is a common thing in almost all the villages of India. As a rule, the Brahmins and other Sivites do not join in this pastime, but all other classes take great delight in it. The fighting cocks are of two kinds —the country breed and the Moghul breed. The Moghul breeds are fine, strong, well-made birds. They are kept in separate places, and not allowed to see each other. If a villager is a well-to-do man, he keeps five or six of these cocks. If he is a big landlord, he keeps about a dozen, and he engages a special man to look after them. His duty it is to feed them both morning and evening, and to give them water at noon. Besides this, he must spend ten or fifteen minutes with each cock in the evening in wetting their necks well with cold water, and specially in pressing with both his hands the neck of each cock. He takes each cock to the tank, and dips its whole body well into the water, and lets it swim for awhile. This kind of preparation goes on for some time before the owner ventures to take them to the fighting-ground. The country breeds are also prepared in the same manner, with the exception of the rubbing of the necks.

The spot for the fighting will be fixed according to the convenience of the villagers. The parties always choose a place where there is plenty of water and shade, and as far as possible away from a village. To this fighting amusement the fair sex do not go, but the men of all ages are exceedingly fond of it. Some of them journey miles in order to attend such scenes. The fight commences at ten o'clock in the morning. A pair of cocks is set up. Each of these belongs to a different party, and generally they do not care to fix matches between cocks of the same village. One of these fights is known as *Vattoopore*; the other is called *Kathypore.* In the former the cocks are engaged in fighting without having any double-edged, small knife attached to their right legs; but in the latter kind they have the knives, and this makes it a most terrible and cruel scene. Soon after these cocks are set up, they severely wound each other, and when one of them dies or runs away, the fight is considered to be ended. The defeated cock is always presented to the owner of the conqueror. In the case of the fighting without knives, one of the cocks must either die or run away. The owner of the cock which conquers its opponent is entitled to the defeated cock, or to a certain sum of money. This kind of amusement sometimes brings great rows, with fighting and loss of money to the owners of these cocks. If a man in a village has a champion cock, it rouses the envy of the people of other villages, who spend a lot of money in purchasing a proper match to it. There is a great deal of skill shown by the men who catch the cocks with knives, even while they are flying against each other.

Sometimes the men are severely wounded while thus attempting to catch the cocks. This must be regarded as a most cruel and degrading way of getting amusement.

There is another kind of village amusement. It is the ram-fight. Poor harmless lambs are taken from the bosom of the shepherds, and are reared by the pleasure-seekers of the village for a considerable time. Some of them teach these rams particular signs, to help them in fighting. This amusement also is solely intended for the *men* of the village, who assemble in large numbers under the shade of the trees. When the parties meet for this purpose they bet large sums of money, which are usually given to the owner of the ram that conquers.

In one of these ram-fights there was a Mohammedan who brought a ram to fight with a ram of a Hindu. There was a large number of spectators to see this fun. The Hindu had his own party of people, and the Mohammedan had his. They met in a fine shady place away from the village, and set their rams to fight at about eight o'clock in the morning. Two of the rams had a previous reputation. The one belonging to the Mohammedan was, indeed, a champion ram. They fought their battle courageously till four o'clock in the evening. The fight was so terrible that the creatures were bleeding from the nose and the ears. Pieces of skin from their heads flew about, and drops of blood fell continually to the earth. Yet neither of these rams showed its back to its rival. At last, the Mohammedan's ram lost one of its horns, and became very weary, and presently fell to the ground facing its enemy. The Hindu's ram was also almost helpless, and was standing in its position facing its enemy. The Mohammedan, who saw his ram broken down, and without strength, spoke to it encouraging and cheering words. As soon as the ram heard the comforting, encouraging, and strengthening voice of its master it stood up on its legs, and with greatly revived spirit and renewed strength fell upon its enemy and fought desperately for ten minutes more, then fell down helpless on the ground. But he heard the voice saying, 'Go on!' 'Get up!' 'Fight!' 'Courage, courage!' from his master. This voice, to the surprise of the spectators, and the man himself, gave new strength to the fallen ram, who rose again, and made another desperate fight. The conflict was so severe that the Hindu had to force the Mohammedan not to speak a word again to the ram.

So the signs and voices with which the rams are trained help them to fight to the very last. Some of the big Zamindars and landowners have ruined themselves by the madness of this ram-fight. We regard the fact with supreme sorrow, that some of our own relations have ruined themselves through this evil habit.

2. SPORTS.

That Turanian blood runs in the veins of the South Indian villagers is a fact which cannot be denied. Although these mountaineers now live in the fertile plains, yet their fondness for hunting, their readiness to endure a jungle life, and their love for the bow and arrow of their ancestors, betray their original mode of living in the high mountains, wild jungles, and thick forests. Their natural love of hunting even now makes them at times leave their ploughs, their home comforts, and their businesses, and betake them to the forest reserves of the Zamindars, or to the rough hills and deep valleys, in order to hunt for wild animals. This habit makes even the poorer villager equip himself with a *kurattookamboo*, *i.e.*, a short stick with iron rings, which is thrown at the animals, and with a dog. Some of them have matchlocks, bows, and spears. These hunting-weapons are used only in the forests of the plains, and in the mountains.

The hounds which the villagers have belong to three different breeds: the Polygar dogs, the Persian breeds, and the Pariah breeds. The Polygar dogs are of medium size, well-built, with strong legs, projecting ears, and firm heads. They are swift in running, and courageous in attacking any animal, and they are very watchful, sensible, and faithful. The Persian dogs are in breeding mixed with the Polygar. Their height and length of body, their thin long head and folded ears, their gentle and beautiful appearance, and their thin tail and soft hair, are very attractive. They are swift in running, and very quick in catching animals, but furious when they are wild. The Pariah breeds are short, ill-made, ugly-looking, dirty, emaciated and cowardly. This dog does not stick to any particular home, and therefore knows no one to call his master. It often barks at people, and is troublesome, slow, and dull-looking. All these three breeds are to be found in the villages.

On high days and holidays a number of men will join together and set out to hunt in the nearest forest reserves. They start very early in the morning, after taking their morning meal, each of them having a dog or two leashed in a thong made out of palmgrass fibre. They also carry a short stick in their hands. Those who have the matchlock or the spear do not have any dogs in their care. As they march on towards the forest they arrange among themselves to leave a few of their number here and there outside the forest, watching for the movements of the animals. The majority of this hunting party go on into the forest, and beat the bushes from one end of it to the other. As they march on they disturb hare, deer, and jackals, and these animals run hither and thither. They set the dogs to pursue and so kill many of them. If there is a chance they shoot the animals. Some of these men, being skilled sportsmen, throw their short and stout sticks at the animals as they run past, and they often either break their legs or kill them on the spot. At about twelve o'clock they all assemble at one end of the forest, in order to quench their thirst and that of their dogs. They are specially careful to wet the bodies of their dogs, so as to enable them to bear the heat of the day. The men take with them no food to eat while they are hunting. All that they ever take with them is a piece of jaggry, which they swallow, and they drink spring-water. This tiffin suffices to give them strength to run after the animals during the remainder of the day. Some of them take a small quantity of jaggry and dried ginger pounded together, and this is considered the best refreshment they can have. In the evening each set of villagers assemble separately, and share the game. If five of them from one village killed five hares, and the whole party from that village were fifty, they equally share among themselves, without any ill-feeling or grudge.

The villagers who live at the foot of the mountains take delight in hunting tigers, hogs, and sometimes elephants. For hog-hunting the villagers set out during the moonlight, taking with them strong and specially selected dogs, match-locks, spears, and big knives, for they do not know at what moment they may meet with a man-eater (tiger). The hogs often come to the cultivated fields near the mountains, and do great damage to the farmers' crops by rooting up the soil. The hunters hide themselves in the bushes and watch these hogs. When the hogs return from the fields one by one they set the dogs on them. A large number of these surround the hogs, and they frequently break the legs of the dogs, or smash their heads, or tear their breasts; but the dogs will not let the hogs escape easily. Some of them catch hold of the hind-legs of the hog, and keep him from escaping. While a hard struggle is going on between the hogs and the dogs, the hunter runs to the spot, and kills the hog with his long spear. The hunting of hogs is considered manly work, for sometimes the hunters lose their lives, or get severe wounds in this sport. While they are hunting the hogs they may suddenly meet with a tiger, which they face manfully and try to kill.

Tiger-hunting is very frequent with those who live in the hill tracts. They go in large numbers, taking their guns, drums, trumpets, knives, and spears; but they do not take their dogs with them. Those who have the guns climb the trees near the forests, and all the others go into the forest and drive the animals by beating the drums and blowing the horns. The tigers, when they hear all this disturbance at a distance of four or five miles, begin to move towards other parts of the forest. When the deer, spotted deer, and antelopes begin to leave their places in advance, their movements are a sure sign that the tigers will follow, so those men who are in the trees in different places hold themselves in readiness with their guns, and keep quiet, letting all the other animals pass by one by one. A group of deer run off to escape for their lives. A large number of beautiful spotted deer run in haste to save their lives. The antelopes, lifting and shaking their beautiful heads, run by. Then the cunning jackals, with their stuffed tails, run by.

All this procession of animals having passed, there is half an hour of waiting-time. The hunters on the trees are watching as calmly as possible. Now they see the bushes shaking, and the plants and leaves being crushed by the majestic and dignified walk of the princes of the forest—the tigers. As they advance towards the trees, some of the men lose their courage and presence of mind, and drop their guns, but the men of undaunted courage aim at the man-eater, and fire. If they are smart men, they shoot the tiger in the right spot and kill him at once. If not they only wound him, and then the whole forest is shaken by its roars. If a tiger is killed it is considered as great game. They carry him in procession, some beating drums, some dancing before it, and in such ways rejoicing over the death of this enemy of mankind. Sometimes tigers come to eat a dead bullock or cow which has been tied to a tree. The hunters get into the trees round about the dead animal, and watch night after night. Perhaps on the second or the third night the tiger will put in his appearance, and begin to eat the flesh of the animal, and then the men in the trees quietly take aim and shoot it. In some cases they face the tiger manfully on the plains, standing face to face and struggling with him. We have seen a hunter wrestle thus with a tiger while he was hunting. The half of the left hand of the man was in the mouth of the tiger, and the right leg of the beast was round the back of the man, while the man, with his right hand, was lifting the upper jaw of the tiger. The tiger tried his best to extricate his upper jaw from the hand of the man, but the man held on for about an hour, when another hunter came with his gun and shot the beast.

There was a famous villager who was in the habit of hunting tigers and hogs with his long spear. He killed several tigers and hogs by facing them on the plain. His fame went abroad, so much so that when a tiger was in the district the villagers used to send for him to kill the brute. On one occasion, when this man had just recovered from a serious illness, he was informed that a tiger had killed several sheep in a neighbouring village, and that it was still prowling about there. This news aroused the spirit of the man, who went to the spot where the tiger was, taking, however, along with him his follower, Mullya Naickeen by name. These two stood in the paddy field and saw the tiger coming towards them. As the tiger was approaching, the man told his follower of the weak state of his health, and that he must help him in keeping down the animal after his dagger had gone through the beast's body. The Naick faithfully assured his master that he would jump on the beast before his master, and kill him with his spear. But when the animal came near them the Naick began to shiver with fear, and altogether lost his presence of mind. The 'mighty hunter' speared the beast, and jumped to the other side of the animal; but the Naick struck his spear into the embankment and then fainted away. After the tiger was killed the Naick was awakened from his unconscious state.

3. ATHLETIC EXERCISES.

Most villagers are a quiet and unwarlike race, but they have several kinds of athletic exercise. They have both outdoor exercises and indoor exercises. Although there is no society or club to promote their physical interest, yet their lads and young men are regularly and actively engaged in these bodily trainings.

There is an exercise called *killitattoo.* Several straight lines are made in the sand with the foot, leaving eight or ten yards between each line, and those who are assembled for the play are divided into two parties, the one advancing, the other opposing. They advance by standing in a regular row. The party who oppose the advance elect the best among them to be their leader, and he is called *killi.* This *killi* always stands on the last line, and watches the movement of the advancing party. This is really a running game. It is often played in the evenings and in moonlight nights. Generally they choose one of the village commons as their play-ground. In this, and other games, the villagers observe a certain amount of regularity and rule, though they have nothing to pay for it.

They also play a kind of cricket at all seasons, but not in the refined and orderly way with which Westerns are familiar. All the villagers who assemble on the play-ground stand on one side, and allow one man to hold both the bat and ball; he strikes it in such a way that it may rise to a great height, in order to give a chance to the people to catch it as it comes down. Whoever catches the ball becomes the striker, so the game really resembles somewhat the English 'catch-out.'

There is another open-air exercise, called *gudoo-gudoo.* It resembles to a great extent the football of Britain. Two parties meet on the common, and separate themselves by a line drawn on the earth. One takes the lead, by sending one of his men to cross the line, and touch one of the opponents, without being caught by him. While he is doing this he must utter, without taking breath, the words '*gudoo, gudoo.*' If he cannot hold his breath, and repeat

THE WRESTLER (*Vasthath*).

'*gudoo, gudoo*' until he crosses the line that divides the parties, he is considered as a 'dead' man on the field, and he is not allowed to play again till one of his party gains.

There is another exercise called *manthy*. This is one of the difficult village games. Men assemble on the grassy plains, and divide themselves into two parties, and adopt the same rules as in playing *killitattoo*; only each of them sits on his legs, and passes his two arms between the legs and grasps his feet, and then he runs like a kangaroo. It is in this play that some break their teeth, or smash their heads against the earth, or hurt their legs or hands. Nevertheless, this play is still loved and practised in all the villages.

There is yet another exercise, called *silambam*, which is both an exercise and an art of offence and defence. There are teachers who give instructions in this art, and some ot them are very clever men. Those who wish to learn this exercise must pay some money or grain to the teacher. Some of these teachers have a large number of pupils under them, and they meet either in the night or very early in the morning, in some lonely place. Each of the pupils must have a long and strong stick in his hand, and the teacher has a similar one, with which he instructs the pupils how to twirl the stick about in defending or in attacking. In twirling the stick there is a great deal of cleverness displayed. This art of *silambam* was originally taught to the warriors of ancient times.

The villagers have still another exercise called *thelloo*, or 'round and black seeds.' This is played in the open fields with the fingers. The principle is more or less the same as in marble playing, but the methods adopted are somewhat different.

4. GAMBLING.

The villagers, being mostly of the agricultural class, cannot find much time for gambling. But the idle, and also the well-to-do among them, both men and women, do often spend their time in this way. The most popular game is known as *Thayam.* This is played by splitting tamarind seed, and making about forty-eight or fifty files on the floor. On these each party has a row of small stones, or broken pieces of earthen vessels. Each party make a move according to the number they get by throwing these tamarind seeds. Their men must go on each other's files on the way they take their opponents. However, there is not much skill in this game.

There is another game which is commonly played by the fair sex, and this is called *pandy.* Eight or ten holes are made on each side of a plank. The parties who play this game each try to fill these holes with five tamarind seeds, so that they make a pile. They commence to play with seeds of one pile; and again they take the seeds of the pile on which the last seed fell. They repeat the process until they come to an empty pile on which they have no seed to place. If they have the last seed to place in it, then the opposite party commences to play, otherwise the party who met the first empty hole takes all the seeds contained in the pile next to the empty one. In this way they reduce each other's seeds. When all the seeds are taken from one side the game is ended. The party who has the largest number of seeds is considered to have won the game.

There is another game which is called *ottay-rattay.* This is played by both sexes. Taking a handful of tamarind seeds, or telloo, and holding the hand closed, one asks the other whether it is odd or even. If the party says that it is odd, while it is really even, then the party who holds the seeds gets an equal number of seeds from the other, otherwise they are taken by the opposite party.

There is another most intellectual and thoughtful game, called *pathinaynthoo nay and puli*, which means 'fifteen dogs and tigers.' This is really the village chess. One man takes the fifteen dogs, that is fifteen small stones, and keeps them in his hand. His opponent takes three small pieces of earthen vessel, and keeps them on the top of certain lines that are drawn on the floor, thus:

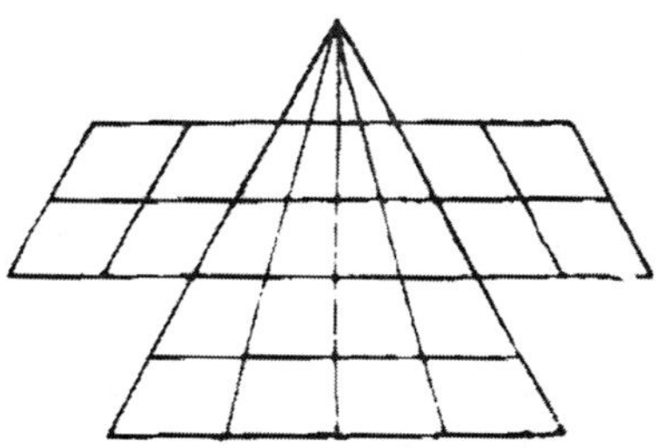

It is the duty of the man who holds the dogs to arrest the tigers without making any further move, and at the same time he must take care that his dogs are not killed by the tigers. Some clever men arrest the tigers by playing only a few dogs, while others lose all the dogs and fail to arrest the tigers. Some of the villagers are very fond of this game. While the two are playing, several others will be watching with great interest.

5. THE FAIR.

There is nothing so useful, nothing so needful to the villagers, as the institution of the village fair, which meets the needs of both the rich and the poor of the village community. Although every village has a *bazaar* of its own, where curry-stuff, eatables, and provisions are sold to supply the daily requirements, yet it is absolutely necessary to have a fair for the reasons which we propose to explain.

There are hundreds of village fairs held throughout the length and breadth of the country. A suitable and convenient centre is chosen, to which the people from different villages, within twenty miles circumference, assemble at about seven o'clock in the morning to sell their goods and to purchase what is necessary for themselves. The dealers in goods come very early in the morning, and open out their petty *bazaars* on plains, either under some trees, or the shade of a country umbrella, or in the temporary sheds that are erected by private parties to whom they pay a small rent for privilege of occupation.

The fairs are held outside the village, where there is a sufficient water-supply for the men and cattle, and where there is a stretch of plain without any enclosure. These fairs are held once a week in each centre, and they last for twelve hours. When we enter the fair we find a sea of heads moving up and down; men and women of all sorts and conditions will be there. In one part will be rows of green vegetables of all kinds; then great heaps of different kinds of grain, the staple food of the villagers. There will also be bags of all sorts of pulse and horse grain. Turning from these, we find bundles of straw and grass kept ready for cattle, and then a row of cloth merchants with different-coloured cloth bundles for the use of men and women and boys and girls. There are also baskets of eatables kept by women in the centre of the fair. Curry-stuff of all kinds, tamarind, sugar, jaggery, salt, nuts, betel leaves, and fruits are in abundance. There are rows of mats made of palm-leaves and grasses, and pillows stuffed with cotton, which forms the bed of the villager. Our eyes are dazzled, and our minds are puzzled, with looking at all these petty shops which are opened upon out-spread carpets. These shops contain other useful articles, such as combs, feeding-bottles, beads, knives, marbles, brass and lead jewels for the lower orders, and other things. And these movable shops are owned by a class of people called *Lubbays*, a low class of Hindus who embraced Islam during the oppression of Tippu Sultan. This community has now become very enterprising and hardworking. There are many bullock-bandies (or carts) standing both outside and within the fair, which have brought the above-described articles.

Buying and selling in a fair is a great art in itself, for the buyers are sure to try to cheat the sellers, and the sellers are equally anxious to cheat the buyers; and both the buyer and the seller will be duped by the middleman. When we take a general glance at one of these movable shops, we find a good number of people waiting at it, some standing and some sitting, some taking an article and turning it up and down to see whether it is good or bad, some asking the price of this or that particular article which they wish to buy, some begging the shopkeeper to reduce the price, some paying a less sum of money than the price fixed by the shopkeeper, and here a row takes place between the buyer and the seller, the former trying to walk away with the article, and on being detected begging the pardon of the seller; some finding fault with the seller for selling a bad or broken article on the last market-day; some moving from place to place to find out where the best and the cheapest can be had; some asking the seller the price of this article, and some asking him to let them know the lowest value of that article. While the buyers and sellers are in this state, the beggars pass through the crowd hither and thither, beating their drums and singing their songs. The red-turbaned policemen are pushing about, exerting their authority, and frightening the ignorant people, not only to keep the place in order, but chiefly to help themselves by way of greasing their palms. When a man or a woman gets tired of driving bargains, he or she may listen to the sweet voice of the harmless shepherd girls, who are calling out, '*more, more,*' *i.e.*, 'buttermilk, buttermilk,' or '*thire, thire,*' *i.e.*, 'curd, curd,' to quench their thirst and to refresh themselves. Having passed the open place where the bulk of the people are engaged in dealing with general goods, we find a few yards away a busy cattle market, where sheep, goats and buffaloes are sold. The sellers, buyers, and brokers are having a hard time of it under the burning sun; and therefore we find a great deal of noise, uproar, confusion, and disorder prevailing. After twelve hours are passed, there is no more selling or buying; there is no voice of man, or woman, or beast to be heard; there is no smelling of the flowers, or the singing of beggars. The *bazaars* are closed and removed from their places, the moving shops are gone; in short, the day has gone and the night has approached, the village fair is closed—all has disappeared. The Hindu poets have compared the present world and all its enjoyments to the 'assembly at a fair'; and John Bunyan, the immortal dreamer, has compared the activity, the common life, and the pleasures of this world, to 'Vanity Fair.'

The village fair is of great advantage to the poor as well as to the rich. The poor buy their weekly supply of grain, and curry stuffs, and the rich avail themselves of the opportunity to get other needful things for themselves. The shoemaker brings his shoes, and buys his food at the fair; the poor women who work at their own hand-spinning machine (the *raht*) sell their thread, and with the money buy the necessaries of life. The flower-seller sells his flowers, which will wither away in the evening, and with the proceeds meet his own demand. The arrangements made to fix these fairs are very efficient. They are usually held on the Mondays in Ramanad, on Wednesdays in Pallanathame, on Saturdays in other places, each at a distance of twenty miles; on the other days they are held somewhere else. So the fairs give a good chance to the petty merchants, who keep shifting their movable stalls from place to place.

Whatever may be the advantages and disadvantages of these village fairs, there is one very noticeable fact in connection with them: the things are sold at a cheaper rate than at the local bazaars of the villages, and things which cannot be had in the village bazaars can be purchased at the fairs. They also afford an opportunity for supplying the best quality and large quantities of any article that is useful in village family life.

APPENDICES.

THE ATTITUDE OF THE VILLAGERS TOWARDS WESTERN PEOPLE.

NOTHING is more amusing and entertaining to the villagers of India than to see a white person in their midst, whether he comes from Europe or from America, because they very seldom come into contact with European people. The grown-up men, women, and children, rich and poor, are greatly astonished at the dress, colour, language, and mode of living of the Western people. Their simple life and their harmless character cause them to be a great novelty in the eyes of the natives. At the mere appearance in a village of a lady or a gentleman from the Western country, a great crowd of villagers is sure to gather round them; the women who are returning from the watering-places, carrying the water-jars, stare at these white angels with great astonishment. The children, who play in the streets, run after these strangers, and stand before them amazed, and folding their hands, but none of them dare to give any trouble, or throw stones, or make a noise, or behave rudely towards the foreigners. The men of the village receive the strangers who have come among them with great cordiality and reverence, and they are ready to oblige them with any article of food or other things, as far as is in their power. If the foreigner happens to stay in a village, either in a tent (which is the case generally) or in a village inn, he will find several young men waiting his command, and willing to do anything he may please. But the working classes, who earn their food by daily wages, expect to get something from the foreigners when their service is required. In some urgent cases they will, however, help the foreigners without any remuneration.

The life and property of the Westerns are considered as sacred by the village people. When the Westerns go to the villages, with their tents, servants, bullock-carts, horses, and other paraphernalia, the villagers show all kindness, profound respect, and great submission. They are not only ready to oblige the Westerns who pass through their villages with an establishment of their own, but when an unfortunate single European or American happens to pass alone on foot from one city to another in search of employment, they show great hospitality and extreme kindness to them. We know several cases in which such unfortunate individuals have had to pass through the rural districts under great disadvantage, through not knowing the language of the people and not being accustomed to their food. One of these individuals informed us of the manner in which the villagers had treated him. They gave him milk and butter-milk for his breakfast, and cooked rice and vegetable curries for his dinner and supper. And some of them, when they saw him walking on foot, made him ride in their bullock-carts, and helped him thus to go a certain distance on his way. In this manner a Frenchman crossed from Erode to Bangalore, and an Englishman from Madras to Ooty, and other Western people have journeyed from one city to another.

It is not always the case that the villagers have the honour and privilege of seeing Western people as they pass through their villages in the more interior parts of the country. There are very many villages in which Western people have never yet set foot. There are only two classes of European people who pass through their country occasionally. The one is that of the self-denying and energetic missionaries of the West, who go on tours in order to preach the Gospel of peace to the ignorant and benighted people; and the other consists of civil officers of the British Government, such as engineers, survey officers, forest officers, police officers, and revenue officers. Their visits are not very frequent, and when they do happen to visit the villages, they behave with a great deal of 'standoffishness.' But this is a common weakness among such officers; perhaps it is the best thing, too, inasmuch as they take a part in governing the country. But this exclusiveness and reservedness of the European officers does not draw forth the sympathy of the villagers, for, as a rule, they fear to approach these officials when they get to know who they are. If their help is sought by these Western officers, they are usually ready to oblige them. The villagers look upon all Westerns, whether they are Britons, Germans, Americans, Frenchmen, Italians, or Spaniards, as the representatives of the ruling British nation; and the differences that exist among these nationalities is not a matter of concern to the quiet and retired people of India, whose amiable characters and utter ignorance of the geography and history of the world make them submissive to all white people whom they may happen to see.

The attitude of the villagers towards the Westerns is generally favourable, and they are the largest of the communities that form the loyal subjects of the British throne. Their obedience towards any member of the Western community is remarkable. They obey not only the men, but even the women of the West, and they look upon them as, in a way, demi-gods.

The attitude of the villagers towards the Western people is not only to be seen in their spirit of obedience, but also in the spirit of sympathy and in the great affection they have for them. There are tales told about the horrible rule and miserable government of the Mohgul emperors, and the extreme wickedness of the Hindu *maradars* and chiefs, who have destroyed the liberties, stolen the properties, and dishonoured the modesty of their women for centuries together. These tales were told to the village-folk while they are young by their grandmothers. They form an unwritten history in the hearts of the harmless villagers, whose forefathers groaned under the iron yoke of the past tyrannical rulers of India. Whenever they turn the pages of this history of the past governments, they see them stained with the blood of their innocent forefathers, and filled with narratives of the most diabolical and inhuman deeds of the Mohammedan kings and the Hindu rulers. Therefore simple, ignorant, and poor though they are, they are able to distinguish between the peace and liberty and prosperity which they enjoy under the British flag, and the disabilities and wrongs under which their forefathers laboured. Hence they manifest a great love for Western persons, whoever they may be and to whatever country they may belong, thinking that they are *Sirkar Manshal* of the *Rajathee*, *i.e.*, the gentlemen belonging to the Queen's Government. It will not be looked upon as presumption on our part to echo the voice of the village community, and say that they are ready to shed their life-blood, if the time should come, for maintaining the British rule in their midst. The following is from the able pen of our esteemed countryman, Mr. Ahmed Hussain, M.A., B.L.: 'When, some years ago, the newspapers talked of a war between England and Russia, I was in a village in an out-of-the-way corner of a midland district. I remember well what the villagers thought and tried to do then. One morning Hindus and Mohammedans flocked to my tent as the postman brought my newspapers. I cannot describe their excitement. They begged me to read the newspapers, and tell them if the Russians had really invaded Hindustan. I wished to try their patience a little, and asked them what they would do if the rumour were true. They said they would at once hide their jewels and money, and go to the Zillah Collector. "To do what?" I asked. "To fight the Russians," was the unanimous reply. I wished to further test the real motive of their determination. "What matters it to you," said I, "if one foreigner goes out and another comes in?" "Don't say so, sir," answered the headman of the village; "don't say so. Although we all grumble to pay heavy taxes, we would rather have the Englishmen rule us, who do not meddle with our religions, than other foreigners who would forcibly convert us to Christianity"' (quoted from *The Madras Christian College Magazine* of March, 1893, Though they are at times grieved and disturbed by the heavy taxes which they have to pay, yet they can say, in the words of the poet, that they love Britain still; 'her faults are many, but her virtues are not few.' It cannot be denied, knowing them as we do, that the village communities are quite contented, and most affectionate towards the Western people.

The spirit of gratitude towards the Western people is another remarkable attitude of the village community. They often speak of the manifold streams of blessings which run through their country. They know not how the steam-engines draw the loaded railway-waggons and passenger-carriages from place to place as swiftly as a bird. They know not by what means the messages of joy and sorrow are despatched from one country to another, within the twinkling of an eye, through the medium of the electric telegraph. They do not know by what power their relatives and friends are carried away from their land of birth to the distant colonies, in order to make their fortunes, by the steamships. They are quite ignorant of the postal arrangement by which their letters of condolence, and their marriage invitations, and their business communications, run to and fro between the countries far and near at a small cost. It is quite a miracle to them to see the spinning and weaving machines working in different parts of the rural districts. They are unable to understand how the large and well-organized body of civil, military, and judicial functionaries carry out their respective duties in protecting the life and property of the country, and in subduing the evil-doers, and in distributing justice among both the innocent and the guilty. They are not told how the magnificent rivers are crossed by gigantic bridges, and the mighty waters scattered abroad through the lowlands and the highlands, through the hills and the mountains, to the plains and fertile valleys, for the convenience of the inhabitants, and for the agricultural improvement of the land. It is a mystery to them to see the descendants of their slaves, and the offspring of their outcast people becoming the great factors in the ruling machinery of the land. Yet they realize that they have an altogether better time than their forefathers had, and that their present benefits were not even dreamt of by their ancestors. So, in the ordinary conversations of the villagers, they speak of the wonderful changes which have taken place during their time through the noble efforts of the Western people.

THE POWER OF THE GOSPEL IN THE VILLAGES.

The Gospel of goodwill to man and peace on earth was once proclaimed by the angels to the shepherds of Bethlehem, who went abroad spreading the glad tidings of the incarnation of our Lord Jesus Christ. The influence of this Gospel was felt throughout the greater part of the world then known to the Romans before the end of the first century. It has been asserted that the Apostle Thomas, whilst labouring in India, was put to death by Brahmins of Maylypure (St. Thoum), near Madras. The account, however, is unworthy of credit; it arose, probably, from confounding the Apostle with a monk named Thomas, who lived at a much later period.

The Gospel of the Everlasting Son of God seems to have been first brought from Alexandria, which was the greatest and most famous commercial city in the world at the beginning of the Christian era. Here the Evangelist Mark taught a school for preachers for several years. It is supposed that Indian merchants who went to Alexandria from the different parts of India to sell their beautiful silks, muslins, and precious pearls, found there a still greater and much more valuable treasure, 'the Pearl of Great Price'; that is, the Gospel of Christ. These Indian merchants, on their return to their native country, told their relatives and friends that the 'Desire of all Nations' had come.

In the beginning of the second century an earnest appeal was made for Christian teachers to Demetrius, Bishop of Alexandria. Pemtoe, who was a very learned man, was sent to India, and, as far as we know, he was the first missionary to India.

About the fourth century a number of Syrian Christian emigrants settled along the coast of Malabar, south-west of India. They obtained great favour from the Hindu King of Malabar, and freely traded in the country. By-and-by they increased in number and wealth; so much so that they had their own princes to rule over them for centuries together. Their bishops came from Antioch, and they remained Christians faithfully till Vasco da Gama came from Portugal, bringing with him Roman Catholic priests, who soon induced these Christians to become Roman Catholics, and those who refused to accept that faith were severely persecuted.

In 1599 an assembly under Archbishop Menerzes met, and they unanimously ordered all the Syrian prayer-books to be burned. Some of these Christians remained unshaken during the persecution. When liberty was secured by the British flag a great number of them left the Romish Church and formed a new sect of Syrian Christians. These Christians are plain-hearted and simple-minded folks; but their priests need better education in Gospel truths.

The pioneer missionaries of the modern missions have entered different parts of the country from time to time, and have set the Gospel light to shine upon those who sat in darkness and the shadow of death. More than a hundred years elapsed, and millions sterling were spent and many precious lives were lost in this sunny land of ours in the missionary enterprise. There are over thirty-three denominational sects represented in the field, and all of them have had the pleasure of seeing converts from heathenism. There are several villages with chapels, churches, preachers, and teachers, and hundreds of Christians assemble together at the sound of the Sabbath bells to sing the songs of praise to the Redeemer of mankind, and their sons and daughters are brought up in the faith of our Lord and Saviour Jesus Christ. It has a charming effect on anyone who visits these rural churches and observes the simple life of the village Christian community.

One of these numerous village stations situated in Tennevelly, called Meigmamapuram, may be described :—When the Rev. J. Thomas took charge of it the village was not a large one, and had few attractions; it was in the midst of a desert of sand, occupied only by palmyra-trees, castor-oil shrubs, and thorn-bushes, with here and there a banyan-tree marking the road to Trichendur. It had a barren and desolate appearance, and during the season when the land-wind, rushing from the mountains, parches the country and sweeps the falling leaves before it, the village was continually enveloped in clouds of sand and dust. It has now become quite an oasis. Wells have been dug by the hand of labour, and streams pour forth from them in every direction; from the deep sand, vegetables, flowers, and fruit of the very best kind are produced. There you may see the rose and jessamine in their beauty, and the cocoanut-tree in all its gracefulness, and there you may taste the plantain, the grape, the pine-apple having a flavour equal to the finest in India. A lofty and beautiful church, able to contain 2,000 people, has been erected of stone; every Lord's Day it is filled with worshippers, who flock to it from all directions at the sound of the Sabbath bells, and thus the prophecy of Isaiah is fulfilled: 'The wilderness and the solitary place shall be glad for them, and the desert shall rejoice and blossom as the rose.'

There are thousands of villages in which the Gospel of Christ has not yet been preached, and there are millions of villagers who still remain in gross idolatry and superstition, but may we not look beyond present discouragements to the time when the victory shall be won and India become 'Immanuel's Land'? It will be then, as now, filled with the temples dedicated to the living God. It will be thickly populated with worshippers; but they will worship God in spirit and in truth. It will have its highways thronged with pilgrims, but they will be travellers on the way to heaven. It will have its Shastras, but they will be the sacred Scriptures. It will have its songs, but they will be sweet songs of praise to God and to the Lamb. Its fathers and mothers, as numerous as now, will be all Christians; its youths of both sexes will all be taught the lessons of early piety.'

As it is the duty and delight of every Indian Christian who has embraced the ennobling religion of Christ to endeavour to spread the knowledge of the Lord among his countrymen, the author of this book has plunged himself into the streams of Providence, and devotes his time and energy to bringing his fellow-countrymen into the everlasting kingdom of God, and he will join with the poet in singing:

'But the end is not. Look onward,
Much must yet be done;
Millions, yet still unbelieving,
Must be sought and won.

'Disappointments will be waiting—
Satan does his best;
Yet all obstacles must vanish
At our God's behest.'

Elliot Stock, Paternoster Row, London.